FORWARD/COMMENTARY

The National Institute of Standards and Technology (NIST) is a measurement standards laboratory, and a non-regulatory agency of the **United States Department of Commerce**. Its mission is to promote innovation and industrial competitiveness. Founded in 1901, as the National Bureau of Standards, NIST was formed with the mandate to provide standard weights and measures, and to serve as the national physical laboratory for the United States. With a world-class measurement and testing laboratory encompassing a wide range of areas of computer science, mathematics, statistics, and systems engineering, NIST's cybersecurity program supports its overall mission to promote U.S. innovation and industrial competitiveness by advancing measurement science, standards, and related technology through research and development in ways that enhance economic security and improve our quality of life.

The need for cybersecurity standards and best practices that address interoperability, usability and privacy has been shown to be critical for the nation. NIST's cybersecurity programs seek to enable greater development and application of practical, innovative security technologies and methodologies that enhance the country's ability to address current and future computer and information security challenges.

The cybersecurity publications produced by NIST cover a wide range of cybersecurity concepts that are carefully designed to work together to produce a holistic approach to cybersecurity primarily for government agencies and constitute the best practices used by industry. This holistic strategy to cybersecurity covers the gamut of security subjects from development of secure encryption standards for communication and storage of information while at rest to how best to recover from a cyber-attack.

Why buy a book you can download for free?   **We print this so you don't have to.**

Some are available only in electronic media. Some online docs are missing pages or barely legible.

We at 4th Watch Publishing are former government employees, so we know how government employees actually use the standards. When a new standard is released, an engineer prints it out, punches holes and puts it in a 3-ring binder. While this is not a big deal for a 5 or 10-page document, many NIST documents are over 100 pages and printing a large document is a time-consuming effort. So, an engineer that's paid $75 an hour is spending hours simply printing out the tools needed to do the job. That's time that could be better spent doing engineering. We publish these documents so engineers can focus on what they were hired to do – engineering. It's much more cost-effective to just order the latest version from Amazon.com

If there is a standard you would like published, let us know. Our web site is usgovpub.com

Many of our titles are available as eBooks for Kindle, iPad, Nook, remarkable, BOOX, and Sony eReaders. Buy the paperback from Amazon and get Kindle eBook FREE using MATCHBOOK. Go to https://usgovpub.com to learn more.

Why buy an eBook when you can access data on a website for free? HYPERLINKS

Yes, many books are available as a PDF, but not all PDFs are bookmarked? Do you really want to search a 6,500-page PDF document manually? Load our copy onto your Kindle, PC, iPad, Android Tablet, Nook, or iPhone (download the FREE kindle App from the APP Store) and you have an easily searchable copy. Most devices will allow you to easily navigate an ePub to any Chapter. Note that there is a distinction between a Table of Contents and "Page Navigation". Page Navigation refers to a different sort of Table of Contents. Not one appearing as a page in the book, but one that shows up on the device itself when the reader accesses the navigation feature. Readers can click on a navigation link to jump to a Chapter or Subchapter. Once there, most devices allow you to "pinch and zoom" in or out to easily read the text. (Unfortunately, downloading the free sample file at Amazon.com does not include this feature. You have to buy a copy to get that functionality, but as inexpensive as eBooks are, it's worth it.) Kindle allows you to do word search and Page Flip (temporary place holder takes you back when you want to go back and check something). Visit **USGOVPUB.COM** to learn more.

NIST Special Publication 800-57 Part 2
Revision 1

Recommendation for Key Management:

Part 2 – Best Practices for Key Management Organizations

Elaine Barker
William C. Barker

COMPUTER SECURITY

National Institute of
Standards and Technology
U.S. Department of Commerce

NIST Special Publication 800-57 Part 2 Revision 1

Recommendation for Key Management:
Part 2 – Best Practices for Key Management Organizations

Elaine Barker
Computer Security Division
Information Technology Laboratory

William C. Barker
Dakota Consulting
Silver Spring, MD

May 2019

U.S. Department of Commerce
Wilbur L. Ross, Jr., Secretary

National Institute of Standards and Technology
Walter Copan, NIST Director and Under Secretary of Commerce for Standards and Technology

Authority

This publication has been developed by NIST to further its statutory responsibilities under the Federal Information Security Modernization Act (FISMA) of 2014, 44 U.S.C. § 3551 *et seq.*, Public Law (P.L.) 113-283. NIST is responsible for developing information security standards and guidelines, including minimum requirements for federal information systems, but such standards and guidelines shall not apply to national security systems without the express approval of appropriate federal officials exercising policy authority over such systems. This guideline is consistent with the requirements of the Office of Management and Budget (OMB) Circular A-130.

Nothing in this publication should be taken to contradict the standards and guidelines made mandatory and binding on federal agencies by the Secretary of Commerce under statutory authority. Nor should these guidelines be interpreted as altering or superseding the existing authorities of the Secretary of Commerce, Director of the OMB, or any other federal official. This publication may be used by nongovernmental organizations on a voluntary basis and is not subject to copyright in the United States. Attribution would, however, be appreciated by NIST.

National Institute of Standards and Technology Special Publication 800-57 Part 2 Revision 1
Natl. Inst. Stand. Technol. Spec. Publ. 800-57 Part 2, Rev. 1, 91 pages (May 2019)
CODEN: NSPUE2

This publication is available free of charge from:
https://doi.org/10.6028/NIST.SP.800-57pt2r1

Certain commercial entities, equipment, or materials may be identified in this document in order to describe an experimental procedure or concept adequately. Such identification is not intended to imply recommendation or endorsement by NIST, nor is it intended to imply that the entities, materials, or equipment are necessarily the best available for the purpose.

There may be references in this publication to other publications currently under development by NIST in accordance with its assigned statutory responsibilities. The information in this publication, including concepts and methodologies, may be used by federal agencies even before the completion of such companion publications. Thus, until each publication is completed, current requirements, guidelines, and procedures, where they exist, remain operative. For planning and transition purposes, federal agencies may wish to closely follow the development of these new publications by NIST.

Organizations are encouraged to review all draft publications during public comment periods and provide feedback to NIST. Many NIST cybersecurity publications, other than the ones noted above, are available at https://csrc.nist.gov/publications.

Comments on this publication may be submitted to:

National Institute of Standards and Technology
Attn: Computer Security Division, Information Technology Laboratory
100 Bureau Drive (Mail Stop 8930) Gaithersburg, MD 20899-8930
Email: keymanagement@nist.gov

All comments are subject to release under the Freedom of Information Act (FOIA).

Reports on Computer Systems Technology

The Information Technology Laboratory (ITL) at the National Institute of Standards and Technology (NIST) promotes the U.S. economy and public welfare by providing technical leadership for the Nation's measurement and standards infrastructure. ITL develops tests, test methods, reference data, proof of concept implementations, and technical analyses to advance the development and productive use of information technology. ITL's responsibilities include the development of management, administrative, technical, and physical standards and guidelines for the cost-effective security and privacy of other than national security-related information in federal information systems. The Special Publication 800-series reports on ITL's research, guidelines, and outreach efforts in information system security, and its collaborative activities with industry, government, and academic organizations.

Abstract

NIST Special Publication (SP) 800-57 provides cryptographic key management guidance. It consists of three parts. Part 1 provides general guidance and best practices for the management of cryptographic keying material. Part 2 provides guidance on policy and security planning requirements. Finally, Part 3 provides guidance when using the cryptographic features of current systems. Part 2 (this document) 1) identifies the concepts, functions and elements common to effective systems for the management of symmetric and asymmetric keys; 2) identifies the security planning requirements and documentation necessary for effective institutional key management; 3) describes Key Management Specification requirements; 4) describes cryptographic Key Management Policy documentation that is needed by organizations that use cryptography; and 5) describes Key Management Practice Statement requirements. Appendices provide examples of some key management infrastructures and supplemental documentation and planning materials.

Keywords

authentication; authorization; availability; backup; certification authority; compromise; confidentiality; cryptographic key; cryptographic module; digital signatures; encryption; integrity; inventory management; key information; key management; cryptographic Key Management Policy; key recovery; private key; public key; public key infrastructure; security plan; symmetric key.

Acknowledgements

The National Institute of Standards and Technology (NIST) gratefully acknowledges and appreciates contributions by Lydia Zieglar from the National Security Agency and Paul Turner from Venafi concerning the many security issues associated with this Recommendation, and by Tim Polk, Bill Burr, and Miles Smid who co-authored the first edition of this publication. NIST also thanks the many contributors from both the public and private sectors whose thoughtful and constructive comments improved the quality and usefulness of this publication.

Table of Contents

1. Introduction

Cryptographic mechanisms are often used to protect the integrity and confidentiality of data that is sensitive, has a high value, or is vulnerable to unauthorized disclosure or undetected modification during transmission or while in storage. A cryptographic mechanism relies upon two basic components: an algorithm (or cryptographic methodology) and a variable cryptographic key. The algorithm and key are used together to apply cryptographic protection to data (e.g., to encrypt the data or to generate a digital signature) and to remove or check the protection (e.g., to decrypt the encrypted data or to verify a digital signature). This is analogous to a physical safe that can be opened only with the correct combination.

Two types of cryptographic algorithms are in common use today: symmetric key algorithms and asymmetric key algorithms. Symmetric key algorithms (sometimes called secret key algorithms) use a single key to both apply cryptographic protection and to remove or check the protection. Asymmetric key algorithms (often called public key algorithms) use a pair of keys (i.e., a key pair): a public key and a private key that are mathematically related to each other. In the case of symmetric key algorithms, the single key must be kept secret from everyone and everything not specifically authorized to access the information being protected. In asymmetric key cryptography, only one key in the key pair, the private key, must be kept secret; the other key can be made public. Symmetric key cryptography is most often used to protect the confidentiality of information or to authenticate the integrity of that information. Asymmetric key cryptography is commonly used to protect the integrity and authenticity of information and to establish symmetric keys.

Given differences in the nature of symmetric and asymmetric key cryptography and of the requirements of different security applications of cryptography, specific key management requirements and methods necessarily vary from application to application. Regardless of the algorithm or application, if cryptography is to deliver confidentiality, integrity, or authenticity, users and systems need to have assurance that the key is authentic, that it belongs to the entity with whom or which it is asserted to be associated, and that it has not been accessed by an unauthorized third party. SP 800-57, *Recommendation for Key Management* (hereafter referred to as SP 800-57 or the Recommendation), provides guidelines and best practices for achieving this necessary assurance.

SP 800-57 consists of three parts. This publication is Part 2 of the Recommendation (i.e., SP 800-57 Part 2 – *Best Practices for Key Management Organizations*) and is intended primarily to address the needs of U.S. government system owners and managers who are setting up or acquiring cryptographic key management capabilities. Parts 1 and 3 of SP 800-57 focus on cryptographic key management mechanisms. SP 800-57 Part 1, *General*, (hereafter referred to as Part 1) contains basic key management guidance intended to advise users, developers and system managers; and SP 800-57 Part 3, *Application-Specific Key Management Guidance*, (hereafter referred to as Part 3) is intended to address specific key management issues associated with currently available implementations.

SP 800-57 has been developed by and for the U.S. Federal Government. Non-governmental organizations may voluntarily choose to follow the practices provided herein.

1.1 Scope

This publication (hereafter referred to as *Part 2*) 1) identifies concepts, functions, and elements that should be common to cryptographic key management systems (CKMS); 2) identifies the security planning requirements and documentation necessary to effective organizational key management; and 3) describes cryptographic Key Management Policy and practice documentation and Key Management Specifications that are needed by organizations that use cryptography. Although there are distinctions between symmetric and asymmetric key management requirements, there is an extensive set of management principles and organizational requirements that are common to both. This publication presents common key management requirements and identifies distinct symmetric algorithm-specific and asymmetric algorithm-specific requirements, when appropriate. This publication also makes recommendations to enterprise organizations for the management of cryptographic keys, the management of metadata associated with those keys (e.g., identifying information associated with the owners of keys, the lengths of keys, and acceptable uses for those keys), and the maintenance of associations between metadata and keys.

This publication is intended to acquaint system owners and managers of organizations implementing and using cryptography with the requirements that must be satisfied when cryptography is implemented in their organizations. It does not address specific key management protocols, implementations, or the operation of key management components or systems. It focuses on principles and requirements that will need to be met by the key management protocols, components, systems and services used by organizations. Key management protocols are documented and coordinated rules for exchanging keys and metadata (e.g., in X.509 certificates). Key management components include the software module applications and hardware security modules (HSMs) that are used to generate, establish, distribute, store, account for, suspend, revoke, or destroy cryptographic keys and metadata.

Cryptographic key management systems (CKMS) are composed of individual components and are used to carry out sets of key management functions or services. Key management services include the generation, destruction, revocation, distribution, and recovery of keys. Some CKMS services (e.g., certificate authority (CA)) may be provided by a third party under contract or Service Level Agreement.

This document identifies applicable laws and directives concerning security planning and management and suggests approaches to satisfying those laws and directives with a view to minimizing the impact of the management overhead on organizational resources and efficiency. Part 2 also acknowledges that planning and documentation requirements associated with small-scale or single-system organizations will not need to be as elaborate as those required for large and diverse government agencies that are supported by multiple information technology systems. However, any organization that employs cryptography to provide security services needs to have key management policy, practices and planning documentation.

Part 2 recognizes that some key management functions, such as the provisioning and revocation of keys, are sufficiently labor-intensive that they act as an impediment to the adoption of cryptographic mechanisms – particularly in large network operations. Nevertheless, responsible key management is essential to the effective use of cryptographic mechanisms for protecting information technology systems against attacks that threaten the confidentiality of the information processed, stored, and communicated; the integrity of information and systems operation; and the timely availability of critical information and services. Improved tools for the automation of many

2

key management services are needed to improve the security, performance, and usability of CKMSs, but the characteristics identified in SP 800-57 as essential to secure and effective key management are valid and independent of performance and usability concerns.

1.2   Audience

The primary audience for Part 2 is the set of federal government system owners and managers who are setting up or acquiring cryptographic key management capabilities. However, consistent with the Cybersecurity Enhancement Act of 2014 (PL 113-274), this Recommendation is also intended to provide cybersecurity guidelines to the private sector in addition to the government-focused guidance consistent with Office of Management and Budget (OMB) Circular A-130 (OMB 130[1]). Since guidelines and best practices for the private sector are strictly voluntary, the requirement terms (i.e., the **should/shall** language) used for some recommendations and requirements do not apply outside the federal government. For federal government organizations, the terms **should** and **shall** have the following meaning in this document:

1. **shall**: This term is used to indicate a requirement for U. S. Federal government organizations based on a Federal Information Processing Standard (FIPS) or NIST Recommendation. Note that **shall** may be coupled with **not** to become **shall not**.

2. **should**: This term is used to indicate an important recommendation. Ignoring the recommendation could result in undesirable results. Note that **should** may be coupled with **not** to become **should not**.

1.3   Background and Rationale

As stated above, although there are significant differences in key management requirements for symmetric and asymmetric key management applications, there are principles common to both. The proper handling of and accounting for keys is necessary for cryptographic functions to be effective. For example, regardless of the cryptographic method employed, some secret or private keys will need to be made available to some set of the entities that use cryptography. Trust in the source of these keys is essential to any confidence in the cryptographic mechanisms being employed. Access to the private or secret keys by entities that are not intended to use them invalidates any assumptions regarding the confidentiality or integrity of information believed to be protected by the associated cryptographic mechanisms. Although organizations may generate keys for their members and distribute keys to their members, the only way to completely protect information being stored under a cryptographic key is for the entity(ies) responsible for storing the information to control the generation, distribution, and key storage processes.

An example of the fundamental differences between the protection requirements for symmetric keys and those for asymmetric keys is that, in the symmetric case, each party that is authorized to use a (secret) key must protect that key in order to avoid all of the parties who also share the key from losing the cryptographic protection afforded under that key. In the asymmetric case, only the party that owns and is authorized to use the private key must protect the confidentiality of that key; the other key of the key pair – the public key – may be known by anyone, but its ownership must n be verified in a trusted manner. However, it is essential in both cases to keep track of

---

[1] OMB A-130, *Managing Information as a Strategic Resource.*

cryptographic keys in use across an enterprise. Information regarding the compromise of a secret or private key or regarding its revocation for any reason must be available to all parties reliant on the security services that use the key.

At the device or software application level, keys need to be provided, changed, and protected in a manner that enables cryptographic operation and preserves the integrity of cryptographic processes and their dependent services. FIPS 140[2] provides guidance on implementing cryptography into a cryptographic module. Other government publications that specify technical key management requirements for specific applications include:

a) SP 800-56A, *Recommendation for Pair-Wise Key Establishment Schemes Using Discrete Logarithm Cryptography*;

b) SP 800-56B, *Recommendation for Pair-Wise Key Establishment Schemes Using Integer Factorization Cryptography*;

c) SP 800-56C, *Recommendation for Key Derivation Methods in Key-Establishment Schemes*;

d) SP 800-71, *Recommendation for Key Establishment Using Symmetric Block Ciphers*;

e) SP 800-108, *Recommendation for Key Derivation Using Pseudorandom Functions*;

f) SP 800-131A, *Transitioning the Use of Cryptographic Algorithms and Key Lengths*;

g) SP 800-132, *Recommendation for Password-Based Key Derivation: Part 1: Storage Applications*;

h) SP 800-133, *Recommendation for Cryptographic Key Generation*; and

i) SP 800-135, *Recommendation for Existing Application-Specific Key Derivation Functions*.

Technical mechanisms alone are not sufficient to ensure the protection of sensitive information. Part 2 specifies key management planning requirements for the development, acquisition, and implementation of cryptographic product and services. In federal government systems, technical mechanisms are required to be used in combination with a set of procedures that implement a clearly understood and articulated protection policy.

In order for key management practices and procedures to be effectively employed, support for these practices and procedures at the highest levels of the organization is a practical necessity. The executive level of the organization needs to establish policies that identify executive-level key management roles and responsibilities for the organization. The key management policies need to support the establishment of, or access to, the services of a key management infrastructure and the employment and enforcement of key management practices and procedures.

1.4 Organization

Part 2 of the *Recommendation for Key Management* is organized as follows:

---

[2] FIPS 140, *Security Requirements for Cryptographic Modules*.

- <u>Section 2</u> introduces key management concepts that must be addressed or understood by organizations that use cryptography to protect information so that they can create key management policies, practice statements and planning documents.

- <u>Section 3</u> provides guidance on planning for the use of cryptography, including the rationale for key management planning.

- <u>Section 4</u> provides information that supports the development of Key Management Specifications by describing the key management components that may be required to operate a cryptographic device or application.

- <u>Section 5</u> and <u>Section 6</u> provide guidance for the development of organizational cryptographic Key Management Policy statements and Key Management Practice Statements. The policy and practice documentation may take the form of separate planning and implementation documents or may be included in an organization's existing information security policies and procedures.[3]

- <u>Appendix A</u> provides cryptographic key management system (CKMS) examples.

- <u>Appendix B</u> provides key management inserts for security plan templates.

- <u>Appendix C</u> provides a Key Management Specification checklist for cryptographic product development.

- <u>Appendix D</u> provides a table of references.

- <u>Appendix E</u> identifies changes from the original SP 800-57 Part 2 document.

1.5 Glossary of Terms and Acronyms

The definitions provided below are consistent with <u>Part 1</u>. Note that the same terms may be defined differently in other documents. Also note that summaries of some of the glossary definitions are used as footnotes throughout the document to assist the reader; the complete definition is provided in Section 1.5.1.

1.5.1 Glossary

Access control	As used in this Recommendation, the set of procedures and/or processes that only allow access to information in accordance with pre-established policies and rules.
Accountability	A property that ensures that the actions of an entity may be traced uniquely to that entity.
Approved	FIPS-Approved and/or NIST-recommended. An algorithm or technique that is either 1) specified in a FIPS or NIST Recommendation, or 2) specified elsewhere and adopted by reference in a FIPS or NIST Recommendation.

---

[3] Agency-wide security program plans are required by OMB guidance on implementing the *Government Information Security Reform Act.*

Archive	See *Key management archive*.
Authentication	A process that provides assurance of the source and integrity of information in communications sessions, messages, documents or stored data or that provides assurance of the identity of an entity interacting with a system.
Authorization	1. Access privileges granted to an entity; conveys an "official" sanction to perform a cryptographic function or other sensitive activity. 2. The process of verifying that a requested action or service is approved for a specific entity.
Availability	Timely, reliable access to information by authorized entities.
Backup	A copy of key information to facilitate recovery during the cryptoperiod of the key, if necessary.
Central Oversight Authority	The cryptographic key management system (CKMS) entity that provides overall CKMS data synchronization and system security oversight for an organization or set of organizations.
Certificate	See *Public key certificate*.
Certificate class	A CA-designation (e.g., "class 0" or "class 1") indicating how thoroughly the CA checked the validity of the certificate. Per X.509 rules, the "class" should be encoded in the certificate as a CP extension: the CA can insert an object identifier (OID) that designates the set of procedures applied for the issuance of the certificate. These OIDs are CA-specific and can be understood only by referring to the CA's Certification Practice Statement.
Certificate owner	The human(s) responsible for the management of a given certificate.
Certificate Policy	A named set of rules that indicate the applicability of a certificate to a particular community and/or class of applications with common security requirements.
Certificate revocation list (CRL)	A list of revoked public key certificates by certificate number that includes the revocation date and (possibly) the reason for their revocation.
Certification Authority (CA)	The entity in a public key infrastructure (PKI) that is responsible for issuing certificates and exacting compliance to a PKI policy.

Certification path	An ordered list of certificates (containing an end-entity subscriber certificate and zero or more intermediate certificates) that enables the receiver to verify that the sender and all intermediate certificates are trustworthy. Each certificate in the path must have been signed by the private key corresponding to the public key contained in the certificate that precedes it in the path, and the first certificate in the path must have been issued by a *Trust anchor*.
Certification Practice Statement	A statement of the practices that a Certification Authority employs in issuing and managing public key certificates.
Ciphertext	Data in its encrypted form.
Client node	An interface for human users, devices, applications and processes to access CKMS functions, including the requesting of certificates and keys.
CKMS component	Any hardware, software, or firmware that is used to implement a CKMS. In this Recommendation, the major CKMS components discussed are the Central Oversight Authority, Key Processing Facilities, Service Agents, Client Nodes and Tokens.
CKMS hierarchy	A system of key processing facilities whereby a key center or certification authority may delegate the authority to issue keys or certificates to subordinate centers or authorities that can, in turn, delegate that authority to their subordinates.
Communicating group	A set of communicating entities that employ cryptographic services and need cryptographic keying relationships to enable cryptographically protected communications.
Compliance audit	A comprehensive review of an organization's adherence to governing documents such as whether a Certification Practice Statement satisfies the requirements of a Certificate Policy and whether an organization adheres to its Certification Practice Statement.
Compromise	The unauthorized disclosure, modification, substitution, or use of sensitive information (e.g., a secret key, private key or secret metadata).
Compromised key list (CKL)	A list of named keys that are known or suspected of being compromised.
Confidentiality	The property that sensitive information is not disclosed to unauthorized entities.
Cross-certification	A process whereby two CAs establish a trust relationship between them by each CA signing a certificate containing the public key of the other CA.

Cryptanalysis	1. Operations performed in defeating cryptographic protection without an initial knowledge of the key employed in providing the protection. 2. The study of mathematical techniques for attempting to defeat cryptographic techniques and information system security. This includes the process of looking for errors or weaknesses in the implementation of an algorithm or of the algorithm itself.
Cryptographic application	An application that performs a cryptographic function.
Cryptographic boundary	An explicitly defined continuous perimeter that establishes the physical bounds of a cryptographic module and contains all the hardware, software, and/or firmware components of a cryptographic module.
Cryptographic device	A physical device that performs a cryptographic function (e.g., random number generation, message authentication, digital signature generation, encryption, or key establishment). A cryptographic device must employ one or more cryptographic modules for cryptographic operations. The device may also be composed from other applications and components in addition to the cryptographic module(s). A cryptographic device may be a stand-alone cryptographic mechanism or a CKMS component.
Cryptographic function	Cryptographic algorithms, together with modes of operation (if appropriate); for example, block ciphers, digital signature algorithms, asymmetric key-establishment algorithms, message authentication codes, hash functions, or random bit generators.
Cryptographic key (key)	A parameter used in conjunction with a cryptographic algorithm that determines its operation in such a way that an entity with knowledge of the key can reproduce or reverse the operation, while an entity without knowledge of the key cannot. Examples include:

- The transformation of plaintext data into ciphertext data,

- The transformation of ciphertext data into plaintext data,

- The computation of a digital signature from data,

- The verification of a digital signature,

- The computation of an authentication code from data,

- The computation of a shared secret that is used to derive keying material.

Cryptographic keying relationship	Two or more entities share the same symmetric key.
Cryptographic Key Management System (CKMS)	The framework and services that provide for the generation, production, establishment, control, accounting, and destruction of cryptographic keys It includes all elements (policies, procedures, devices, and components); facilities; personnel; procedures; standards; and information products that form the system that establishes, manages, and supports cryptographic products and services for end entities. The CKMS may handle symmetric keys, asymmetric keys or both.
Cryptographic mechanism	An element of a cryptographic application, process, module or device that provides a cryptographic service, such as confidentiality, integrity, source authentication, and access control (e.g., encryption and decryption, and digital signature generation and verification).
Cryptographic module	The set of hardware, software, and/or firmware that implements **approved** cryptographic functions (including key generation) that are contained within the cryptographic boundary of the module.
Cryptographic product	Software, hardware or firmware that includes one or more cryptographic functions. A cryptographic product is or contains a cryptographic module.
Cryptographic service	A service that provides confidentiality, integrity, source authentication, entity authentication, non-repudiation support, access control and availability (e.g., encryption and decryption, and digital signature generation and verification).
Cryptoperiod	The time span during which a specific key is authorized for use or in which the keys for a given system or application may remain in effect.
Data integrity	A property whereby data has not been altered in an unauthorized manner since it was created, transmitted, or stored.
Decryption	The process of changing ciphertext into plaintext using a cryptographic algorithm and key.
De-registration (of a key)	The inactivation of the records of a key that was registered by a registration authority.
Destruction	The process of overwriting, erasing, or physically destroying information (e.g., a cryptographic key) so that it cannot be recovered. See SP 800-88.[4]

---

[4] SP 800-88 Revision 1, *Guidelines for Media Sanitization.*

Digital signature	The result of a cryptographic transformation of data that, when properly implemented, provides the services of:
	1. Source/entity authentication,
	2. Data integrity authentication, and/or
	3. Support for signer non-repudiation.
Distribution	See *Key distribution*.
Domain parameters	Parameters used in conjunction with some public-key algorithms to generate key pairs, to create digital signatures, or to establish keying material.
Emergency revocation	A revocation of keying material that is effected in response to an actual or suspected compromise of a key.
Encryption	The process of changing plaintext into ciphertext using a cryptographic algorithm and key.
End entity	An entity that is identified as the subject of a certificate at the end of a certification path or shares a symmetric key with other entities for communication.
Entity	
Ephemeral Key	A cryptographic key that is generated for each execution of a key-establishment process and that meets other requirements of the key type (e.g., unique to each message or session).
Hardware Security Module (HSM)	A physical computing device that safeguards and manages cryptographic keys and provides cryptographic processing. An HSM is or contains a cryptographic module.
Initialization Vector (IV)	A vector used in defining the starting point of a cryptographic process (e.g., encryption and key wrapping).
Installation (of keying material)	The process of making keying material available for establishing and maintaining cryptographic relationships.

Integrity	1. In the general information security context (as defined in SP 800-53 [5]): guarding against improper modification; includes ensuring information non-repudiation and authenticity.
	2. In a cryptographic context: the property that sensitive data has not been modified or deleted in an unauthorized and undetected manner since it was created, transmitted or stored.
	The Internet Engineering Task Force (IETF) protocol (RFC 5996) that is used to set up a security association in the Internet Protocol Security (IPsec) protocol suite.
Kerberos	A network authentication protocol that is designed to provide strong authentication for client/server applications by using symmetric-key cryptography.
Key agreement	A (pair-wise) key-establishment procedure in which the resultant secret keying material is a function of information contributed by both participants so that neither party can predetermine the value of the secret keying material independently from the contributions of the other party. Key agreement includes the creation (i.e., generation) of keying material by the key-agreement participants. A separate distribution of the generated keying material is not performed. Contrast with *Key transport*.
Key center	A common central source of the keys or key components that are necessary to support cryptographically protected exchanges within one or more communicating groups.
Key (or key pair) owner	One or more entities that are authorized to use a symmetric key or the private key of an asymmetric key pair.
Key-center environment	As used in this Recommendation, an environment in which the keys or key components needed to support cryptographically protected exchanges within one or more communicating groups are obtained from a common central source.

---

[5] SP 800-53, *Security and Privacy Controls for Federal Information Systems and Organizations.*

Key component	One of at least two parameters that have the same security properties (e.g., randomness) as a cryptographic key; parameters are combined using an **approved** cryptographic function to form a plaintext cryptographic key before use.
Key derivation	As used in this Recommendation, a method of deriving keying material from a pre-shared key and possibly other information. See SP 800-108.
Key distribution	The transport of key information from one entity (the sender) to one or more other entities (the receivers). The sender may have generated the key information or acquired it from another source as part of a separate process. The key information may be distributed manually or using automated key transport mechanisms.
Key Distribution Center (KDC)	
Key generation	The generation of a cryptographic key either as a single process using a random bit generator and an **approved** set of rules, or as created during key agreement or key derivation.
Key information	Information about a key that includes the keying material and associated metadata relating to the key. See *Keying material* and *Metadata*.
Key management	The activities involved in the handling of cryptographic keys and other related parameters (e.g., IVs and domain parameters) during the entire life cycle of the keys, including their generation, storage, establishment, entry and output into cryptographic modules, use and destruction.
Key management components	The software module applications and hardware security modules (HSMs) that are used to generate, establish, distribute, store, account for, suspend, revoke, or destroy cryptographic keys and metadata.

Key management function	Functions used 1) to establish cryptographic keys, certificates and the information associated with them; 2) for the accounting of all keys and certificates; 3) for key storage and recovery; 4) for revocation and replacement (as needed); and 5) for key destruction.
Key Management Plan	Documents how key management for current and/or planned cryptographic products and services will be implemented to ensure lifecycle key management support for cryptographic processes.
Key management planning documentation	The Key Management Specification, CKMS Security Policy and CKMS Practice Statement
Key Management Policy	A high-level document that identifies a high-level structure, responsibilities, governing standards and guidelines, organizational dependencies and other relationships, and security policies.
Key management product	A symmetric or asymmetric cryptographic key, a public-key certificate and other related items (such as domain parameters, IVs, random numbers, certificate revocation lists and compromised key lists, and tokens) that are obtained by a trusted means from some source.
Key Management Practice Statement	A document or set of documentation that describes (in detail) the organizational structure, responsible roles, and organization rules for the functions identified in the associated cryptographic Key Management Policy (see IETF RFC 3647[6]).
Key management protocol	Documented and coordinated rules for exchanging keys and metadata (e.g., X.509 certificates).
Key management service	The generation, establishment, distribution, destruction, revocation, and recovery of keys.
Key pair	A public key and its corresponding private key. A key pair is used with a public key algorithm.

---

[6] RFC 3647, *Internet X.509 Public Key Infrastructure Certificate Policy and Certification Practices Framework.*

Key processing facility	A CKMS component that performs one or more of the following functions:

- The acquisition or generation of public key certificates,

- The initial establishment of keying material (including its generation and distribution),

- The maintenance of a database that maps end entities to an organization's certificate/key structure,

- Key backup, archiving, inventory or recovery,

- The maintenance and distribution of key compromise lists and/or certificate revocation lists (i.e., Revoked Key Notifications), and

- The generation of audit requests and the processing of audit responses as necessary for the prevention of undetected compromises.

Key recovery	Mechanisms and processes that allow authorized entities to retrieve or reconstruct keys and other key information from key backups or archives.
Key-recovery agent	A human entity authorized to access stored key information in key backups and archives.
Key specification	A specification of the data format, cryptographic algorithms, physical media, and data constraints for keys required by a cryptographic device, application or process.
Key Translation Center (KTC)	
Key wrapping	
Keying material	A cryptographic key and other parameters (e.g., IVs or domain parameters) used with a cryptographic algorithm.

Mesh	A cryptographic checksum based on an **approved** cryptographic function and a symmetric key to detect both accidental and intentional modifications of data.
Metadata	The information associated with a key that describes its specific characteristics, constraints, acceptable uses, ownership, etc. Sometimes called the key's attributes.
Multiple-center group	As used in this Recommendation, a set of two or more key centers that have agreed to work together to provide cryptographic keying services to their subscribers.
Non-repudiation	1. A service using a digital signature that is used to support a determination of whether a message was actually signed by a given entity.
	2. In a general information security context, assurance that the sender of information is provided with proof of delivery, and the recipient is provided with proof of the sender's identity, so neither can later deny having processed the information.
Online Certificate Status Protocol responder	A PKI entity that verifies the revocation status of certificates following the Online Certificate Status Protocol (specified in RFC 6960).
Party	See *Entity*.
Password	A string of characters (letters, numbers and other symbols) that is used to authenticate an identity, to verify access authorization or to derive cryptographic keys.
Peers	Entities at the same tier in a CKMS hierarchy (e.g., all peers are client nodes).
Plaintext	Intelligible data that has meaning and can be understood without the application of decryption.

Private key	A cryptographic key used with a public-key cryptographic algorithm that is uniquely associated with an entity and is not made public. The private key has a corresponding *public key*. Depending on the algorithm, the private key may be used to: 1. Compute the corresponding public key, 2. Compute a digital signature that may be verified by the corresponding public key, 3. Decrypt keys that were encrypted by the corresponding public key, or 4. Compute a shared secret during a key agreement transaction.
Public key	A cryptographic key used with a public-key cryptographic algorithm that is uniquely associated with an entity and that may be made public. The public key has a corresponding *private key*. The public key may be known by anyone and, depending on the algorithm, may be used: 1. To verify a digital signature that is signed by the corresponding private key, 2. To encrypt keys that can be decrypted using the corresponding private key, or 3. As one of the input values to compute a shared secret during a key agreement transaction.
Public key certificate	A set of data that uniquely identifies an entity, contains the entity's public key and possibly other information, and is digitally signed by a trusted party, thereby binding the public key to the entity (e.g., using an X.509 certificate). Additional information in the certificate could specify how the key is used and its validity period.
Public-key (asymmetric) cryptographic algorithm	A cryptographic algorithm that uses two related keys, a *public key* and a *private key*. The two keys have the property that determining the private key from the public key is computationally infeasible.
Public Key Infrastructure (PKI)	A framework that is established to issue, maintain and revoke public key certificates.
Registration authority (RA)	A trusted entity that establishes and vouches for the identity and authorization of a certificate applicant on behalf of some authority (e.g., a CA).

Relying party	An entity that relies on the certificate and the CA that issued the certificate to verify the identity of the certificate's subject and/or owner; the validity of the public key, associated algorithms and any relevant parameters; and the subject's possession of the corresponding private key.
Revocation	A process whereby a notice is made available to affected entities that keys **should** be removed from operational use prior to the end of the established cryptoperiod of those keys.
Revoked key notification (RKN)	A report (e.g., a list) of one or more keys that have been revoked and the date(s) of revocation, possibly along with the reason for their revocation. Certificate Revocation Lists (CRLs) and Compromised Key Lists (CKLs) are examples of RKNs, along with Online Certificate Status Protocol (OCSP) responses (see RFC 6960).[7]
Security policy	A set of criteria for the provision of security services.
Service agent	An intermediate distribution or service facility. Some key management infrastructures may be sufficiently large or support sufficiently organizationally complex organizations that make it impractical for those organizations to receive keying material directly from a common key processing facility.
Source authentication	The process of providing assurance about the source of information. Sometimes called origin authentication. Compare with *Entity authentication*.
Sponsor (of a certificate)	A human entity that is responsible for managing a certificate for the non-human entity identified as the subject in the certificate (e.g., applying for the certificate; generating the key pair; replacing the certificate, when required; and revoking the certificate). Note that a certificate sponsor is also a sponsor of the public key in the certificate and the corresponding private key.
Sponsor (of a key)	A human entity that is responsible for managing a key for the non-human entity (e.g., device, application or process) that is authorized to use the key.
Subject (in a certificate)	The entity authorized to use the private key associated with the public key in the certificate.

---

[7] RFC 6960, *X.509 Internet Public Key Infrastructure Online Certificate Status Protocol – OCSP, Updates.*

Suspension	The process of temporarily changing the status of a key or certificate to invalid (e.g., in order to determine if it has been compromised). The certificate may subsequently be revoked or reactivated.
Symmetric key	A single cryptographic key that is used by one or more entities with a symmetric key algorithm.
Symmetric-key algorithm	A cryptographic algorithm that employs the same secret key for an operation and its complement (e.g., encryption and decryption).
Threat	Any circumstance or event with the potential to adversely impact operations (including mission function, image, or reputation), agency assets or individuals through an information system via unauthorized access, destruction, disclosure, modification of data, and/or denial of service.
Token	A portable, user-controlled, physical device (e.g., smart card or memory stick) used to store cryptographic information and possibly also perform cryptographic functions.
Transport Layer Security (TLS) protocol	An authentication and security protocol that is widely implemented in browsers and web servers. TLS is defined by RFC 5246[8] and RFC 8446.[9] TLS is similar to the older Secure Sockets Layer (SSL) protocol, and TLS 1.0 is effectively SSL version 3.1. SP 800-52[10] specifies how TLS is to be used in government applications.
Trust anchor	
User	A human entity.
Validity period	The period of time during which a certificate is intended to be valid; the period of time between the start date and time and end date and time in a certificate.

---

[8] RFC 5246, *The Transport Layer Security (TLS) Protocol Version 1.2.*

[9] RFC 8446, *The Transport Layer Protocol (TLS) Version 1.3.*

[10] SP 800-52, *Guidelines for the Selection, Configuration, and Use of Transport Layer Security (TLS) Implementations.*

[11] RFC 5914, *Trust Anchor Format.*

| *Wrapped keying material* | Keying material that has been encrypted and its integrity protected using an **approved** key wrapping algorithm and a key wrapping key in order to disguise the value of the underlying plaintext key. |
| *X.509 certificate* | The X.509 public-key certificate or the X.509 attribute certificate, as defined by the ISO/ITU-T[12] X.509 standard. Most commonly (including in this document), an X.509 certificate refers to the X.509 public-key certificate. |

1.5.2 Acronyms

The following abbreviations and acronyms are used in this document:

AES	Advanced Encryption Standard (algorithm)
ASN.1	Abstract Syntax Notation One
CA	Certification Authority
CIO	Chief Information Officer
CKL	Compromised Key List
CKMS	Cryptographic Key Management System
CKMS SP	Cryptographic Key Management System Security Policy
CKMS PS	Cryptographic Key Management System Practice Statement
CPS	Certification Practice Statement
CP	Certificate Policy
CRL	Certificate Revocation List
DH	Diffie Hellman (algorithm)
ECDSA	Elliptic Curve Digital Signature Algorithm
FIPS	Federal Information Processing Standard
GCM	Galois Counter Mode (algorithm)
IETF	Internet Engineering Task Force
IPsec	Internet Protocol Security
IKE	Internet Key Exchange
ISA	Interconnection Service Agreement
ISO	International Standards Organization
ITU	International Telecommunication Union

---

[12] Internalional Standards Organization/International Telecomunication Union-Telecommunication Standardization Sector.

IV	Initialization Vector
KMP	Key Management Policy (See CKMS SP)
KMPS	Key Management Practice Statement (See CKMS PS)
MOA	Memorandum of Agreement
MOU	Memorandum of Understanding
NIST	National Institute of Standards and Technology
OAEP	Optimal Asymmetric Encryption Padding (RSA mode for key transport)
OCSP	Online Certificate Status Protocol
OID	Object Identifier
OMB	Office of Management and Budget
PKI	Public Key Infrastructure
RA	Registration Authority
RSA	Rivest Shamir Adelman (algorithm)
RBG	Random Bit Generator
RKN	Revoked Key Notification
S/MIME	Secure/Multipurpose Internet Mail Exchange (network protocol)
SP	Special Publication
SSH	Secure Shell (network protocol)
TLS	Transport Layer Security
TLS/SSL	Transport Layer Security/Secure Sockets Layer
VPN	Virtual Private Network

2   Key-Management Concepts

This section introduces key-management concepts that must be addressed or understood by any organization that uses cryptography to protect its information so that they can create key-management policies, practice statements and planning documents.

Section 2.1 describes key establishment fundamentals, and Section 2.2 lists basic key management functions. Section 2.3 provides a high-level overview of cryptographic key management systems (CKMS) – the framework and services that provide for the generation, establishment, control, accounting, and destruction of cryptographic keys. Section 2.4 presents general design requirements for a CKMS, and Section 2.5 briefly addresses trust mechanisms. Finally, Section 2.6 addresses the suspension and revocation of keys.

2.1   Key Establishment

Key establishment is the process that results in the sharing of a key between two or more entities. This process could be by a manual distribution, by using automated key-transport or key-agreement mechanisms, or by key derivation using an already-shared key between or among those entities. Key establishment processes include the creation of a key. Key establishment techniques and issues are discussed in Section 5.3 of SP 800-175B.[13]

During key establishment, a decision must be made about the length of each key's cryptoperiod (the length of time that each key may be used). Guidance on the selection of cryptoperiods is provided in Part 1.

2.2   Key-Management Functions

Each key management function needs to be addressed by an organization's cryptographic Key Management Policy. This is true for organizations already using cryptography as well as organizations that do not currently acquire, distribute, use and manage keying material. Key management policies and practices need to be documented (see Sections 5 and 6). Roles and responsibilities need to be defined for the management of at least the following functions:

- The generation or acquisition of key information (i.e., keying material and the associated metadata);
- The secure distribution of private keys, secret keys and the associated metadata;
- The establishment of cryptoperiods;
- Key and/or certificate inventory management, including procedures for the routine supersession of keys and certificates at the end of a cryptoperiod or validity period;
- Procedures for the emergency revocation of compromised keys and the establishment (e.g., distribution) of replacement keys and/or certificates;

---

[13] SP 800-175B, *Guideline for Using Cryptographic Standards in the Federal Government: Cryptographic Mechanisms.*

- Accounting for and the storage and recovery of the operational and backed-up copies of key information;

- The storage and recovery of archived key information;

- Procedures for checking the integrity of stored key information before using it; and

- The destruction of private or secret keys that are no longer required.

2.3 Cryptographic Key Management Systems (CKMS)

The term cryptographic key management system (CKMS) refers to the framework and services that provide for the generation, establishment, control, accounting, and destruction of cryptographic keys and associated management information. It includes all elements (hardware, software, other equipment, and documentation); facilities; personnel; procedures; standards; and information products that form the system that establishes, manages, and supports cryptographic products and services for end entities. A CKMS may handle symmetric keys, asymmetric keys or both.

Key management policies, practice statements, and specifications **should** identify common CKMS elements and suggest functions of and relationships among the organizational elements responsible for the management and use of cryptographic keys. The complexity of a key-management infrastructure and the allocation of roles within a key-management infrastructure will depend on 1) the cryptographic algorithms employed, 2) the operational and communications relationships among the organizational elements being served, 3) the purposes for which cryptography is employed, and 4) the number and complexity of cryptographic keying relationships required by an organization.

The structure, complexity, and scale of CKMSs may vary considerably according to the needs of individual organizations. However, the elements and functions identified in Part 2 need to be present in most organizations that require cryptographic protection. This subsection describes the common CKMS organizational elements, functions, and requirements. Examples of real-world CKMS are provided in Appendix A.

A CKMS is designed to incorporate a set of functional elements that collectively provide unified and seamless protection policy enforcement and key management services.[14] Several distinct functional elements are identified for the generation, establishment, and management of cryptographic keys: a Central Oversight Authority, one or more key processing facility(ies), (optional) service agents, client nodes and (optional) hardware tokens used for entity authentication or initializing keys. It should be noted that organizations may choose to combine the functionality of more than one element into a single component. Figure 1 illustrates functional CKMS relationships.

---

[14] Key management services: The generation, establishment, distribution, destruction, revocation, and recovery of keys.

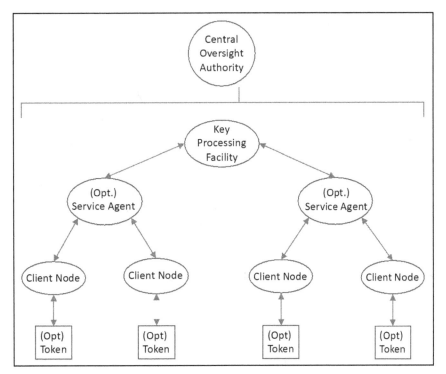

Figure 1: CKMS Components

2.3.1 Central Oversight Authority

As used in this Recommendation, the CKMS's Central Oversight Authority is the entity that provides overall CKMS data synchronization and system security oversight for an organization or set of organizations. The Central Oversight Authority 1) coordinates protection policy and practices (procedures) documentation, 2) may function as a holder of key management information provided by service agents, and 3) serves as the source for common and system-level information required by service agents (e.g., key information and registration information, directory data, system policy specifications, and system-wide key compromise and revocation information). As required by policies for survivability or continuity of operations, Central Oversight Authority facilities may be replicated at an appropriate remote site to function as a system back up.

2.3.2 Key-Processing Facility(ies)

Key-processing facilities are CKMS components that typically provide one or more of the following services:

- Generation and/or distribution of key information;

- Acquisition or generation of public-key certificates (where applicable);

- Backup[15], archiving[16], and inventories[17] of key information;

- Maintenance of a database that maps entities to an organization's certificate or key structure;

- Maintenance and distribution of revoked key or certificate reports (see Section 2.6); and

- Generation of audit requests and the processing of audit responses as necessary for the detection of previously undetected compromises and the analysis of compromise events as needed to support recovery from compromises.

Where public key cryptography is employed, the organization operating the key processing facility will generally perform most PKI registration authority, repository, and archive functions. The organization also performs at least some PKI certification authority functions. Actual X.509 public-key certificates may be obtained from a government source (e.g., certification authorities generating identification or encryption certificates) or a commercial external certification authority (usually a commercial infrastructure/CA that supplies/sells X.509 certificates). Commercial external certification authority certificates **should** be cross-certified by a government root CA.

An organization may use more than one key-processing facility to provide these services (e.g., for inter-organizational interoperation). Key-processing facilities can be added to meet new requirements or deleted when no longer needed, and they may support both public key and symmetric key-establishment techniques.

A key-processing facility may be distributed such that intermediary redistribution facilities maintain stores of keying material that exist in physical form (e.g., magnetic media, smart cards) and may also serve as a source for non-cryptographic products and services (e.g., software downloads for CKMS-reliant entities, usage documents, or policy authority).

Secret and private keys and secret metadata that are electronically distributed to end entities **shall** be wrapped (i.e., encrypted and their integrity protected) for the end entity or for intermediary redistribution services before transmission. Public keys and products not requiring confidentiality protection (e.g., non-secret metadata) that are electronically distributed to end entities **shall** be provided with integrity protection.

Some key-processing facilities may generate and produce human-readable key information and other key-related information that require physical (i.e., manual) distribution. Keys that are manually distributed **shall** either 1) be cryptographically protected in the same manner as those intended for electronic distribution or 2) receive physical protection and be subject to controlled distribution (e.g., registered mail) between the key processing facility and the end entity.

Part 1 provides general guidance for key distribution. Newly deployed key-processing facilities **should** be designed to support legacy and existing system requirements and to support future network services as they become available.

---

[15] Backups are used to store keys for recovery if they become unavailable during their cryptoperiods.

[16] Archives are used for long-term access to keys (e.g., after the cryptoperiods have ended).

[17] Inventories are used for accounting purposes and to look for keys or certificates that have or are about to expire, belong to a particular entity, keys used at a remote location, etc.

2.3.3 Service Agents

Some key-management infrastructures may be large enough or may support sufficiently complex organizations that it is impractical for the organizations to receive key information directly from a common CKMS key-processing facility. Intermediate distribution or service facilities, called *service agents*, may be employed to perform the distribution process.

Service agents, when required by the infrastructure, support an organization's CKMS(s) as single points of access for client nodes. When service agents are used, all transactions initiated by client nodes are either processed by a service agent or forwarded to a key-processing facility. When services are required from multiple key-processing facilities, service agents coordinate services among the key-processing facilities to which they are connected. A service agent that supports a major organizational unit or geographic region may either access a central or inter-organizational key-processing facility or employ local, dedicated processing facilities (e.g., commercial external CAs) as required to support survivability, performance, or availability requirements.

Service agents may be employed by human users or sponsors to order key information and services, retrieve key information, and manage keys and public-key certificates. A service agent may provide key information and/or certificates by utilizing specific key-processing facilities for key and/or certificate generation.

Service agents may provide registration, directory services, support for data-recovery services (i.e., using key recovery), and access to relevant documentation such as policy statements and infrastructure devices. Service agents may also process requests for keying material, assign and manage CKMS roles and privileges, and provide interactive help-desk services.

2.3.4 Client Nodes

Client nodes are interfaces for human users, devices, applications and processes to access key management functions, including the requesting of certificates and keying material. Client nodes may include cryptographic modules, software, and the procedures necessary to provide access to other CKMS components. Client nodes may interact with service agents (when used) or interact directly with key-processing facilities (when service agents are not used) to obtain key management services. Client nodes may interact directly with other client nodes to establish keys (i.e., using key agreement or key transport schemes). Client nodes provide interfaces to end entities for the establishment of keying material, for the generation of requests for keying material, for the receipt and forwarding (as appropriate) of revoked key notifications (RKNs), for the receipt of audit requests, and for the delivery of audit responses.

Client nodes typically initiate requests for keys in order to synchronize new or existing entities with the current key structure and receive wrapped keys for distribution to end entities. A CKMS client node can be a special-purpose device containing a FIPS 140-validated cryptographic module. Actual interactions between a client node and a service agent or a key-processing facility (in the event that a service agent is not used) depend on whether the client node is a device, a functional security application or a computer process.

2.3.5   Tokens

Tokens may be used by human users to interface with their systems that include the CKMS's client node. These tokens typically contain information and keys that allow a human user to interact with their systems by authenticating the user's identity to the system and providing keys for protecting communications. Examples of such tokens are the Federal government's Personal Identity Verification (PIV) cards and Common Access Cards (CAC).

2.3.6   Public Key Infrastructure Environments

A public key infrastructure (PKI) is the combination of software, public key technologies, and services that enables enterprises to protect the security of their communications and business transactions on networks. A PKI integrates digital certificates, public key cryptography, and certification authorities into a complete enterprise-wide network security architecture. A typical enterprise's PKI encompasses the issuance of digital certificates to individual entities; end-entity enrollment software; integration with certificate directories; tools for managing, replacing, and revoking certificates; and related services and support.

The term *public key infrastructure* is derived from public key cryptography, the technology on which a PKI is based. Public key cryptography is the technology behind current digital signature techniques. It has unique features that make it extremely useful as a basis for security functions in distributed systems. A brief discussion of PKIs is provided in Section 5.2.3 of SP 800-175B and in SP 800-32.[18] An example of a PKI is included in Appendix A.1.

2.3.7   Symmetric Key Environments

Symmetric key cryptography requires the originator and all intended consumers of specific information secured by a symmetric-key algorithm to share a secret key. This is in contrast to asymmetric-key (public key) algorithm that requires only one party participating in a transaction to know a private key and permits the other party or parties to know the corresponding public key. Symmetric-key algorithms are generally much more computationally efficient than public key algorithms, so a symmetric-key algorithm is most commonly used to protect larger volumes of information such as the confidentiality of data in transit and in storage. Symmetric-key architectures include center-based architectures and key establishment for communicating groups. While it is possible for pairs of correspondents to employ symmetric-key cryptographic algorithms for wrapping keys they exchange, institutional use of symmetric-key algorithms for key wrapping involves the distribution of keys by a central facility.

SP 800-71 provides discussions on symmetric-key architectures: Key Distribution Centers, Key Translation Centers, Multiple-Center Groups and communicating groups (e.g., peer-to-peer communications).

---

[18] SP 800-32, *Introduction to Public Key Technology and the Federal PKI Infrastructure.*

2.3.8 Hierarchies and Meshes

Multiple key-processing facilities may be organized so that subscribers from different domains may interact with each other. Two common constructions are hierarchies and meshes.

In a CKMS hierarchy, as shown in Figure 2, multiple layers of key-processing facilities may be used, each with its own service agent(s) and client nodes, if appropriate (not shown in the figure). Each layer (except the top layer) is "dominated" in some way by a higher-level key-processing facility.

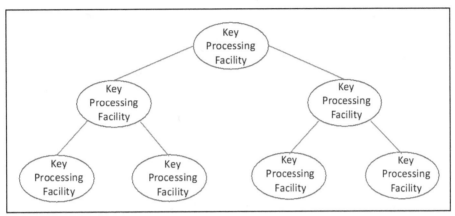

Figure 2: CKMS Hierarchy

In a meshed CKMS architecture, as shown in Figure 3, each key-processing facility may interact with other key-processing facilities in the mesh, but no concept of dominance is implied by the architecture.

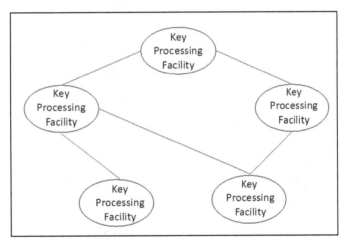

Figure 3: CKMS Mesh Architecture

2.3.9 Centralized vs. Decentralized Infrastructures

A CKMS can be either centralized or decentralized in nature. For a PKI, the public key does not require protection, so decentralized key management can work efficiently for both large-scale and small-scale cases. The management of symmetric keys, particularly for large-scale operations, often employs a centralized structure.

Centralized CKMS key-management structures tend to be more structurally rigid than decentralized key-management structures, but the choice of how to establish keys, store and account for them, maintain an association of keys with the information protected under those keys, and dispose of keys that are no longer needed is a decision to be made by an organization's security management team. Part 1 provides specific guidance regarding constraints associated with each key-management function across the life cycle of keying material.

2.3.10 Available Automated Key Management Schemes and Protocols

Examples of automated key-management systems include IPsec [19] IKE [20] and Kerberos. [21] S/MIME[22] and TLS[23] also include automated key-management functions. The design of key-management schemes is technically very challenging. The most frequent sources of vulnerabilities that result in an adversary defeating cryptographic mechanisms are vulnerabilities in key management (e.g., a failure to change session keys frequently or at all, protocol weaknesses, insecure storage, or insecure transport).

Some examples of IETF standards and guidelines for cryptographic key management include:

- RFC 4210, *Internet X.509 Public Key Infrastructure Certificate Management Protocol (CMP)*

- RFC 4535, *GSAKMP: Group Secure Association Key Management Protocol*

- RFC 4758, *Cryptographic Token Key Initialization*

- RFC 4962, *Guidance for Authentication, Authorization, and Accounting (AAA) Key Management*

- RFC 5083, *Cryptographic Message Syntax (CMS) Authenticated Enveloped-Data Content Type*

- RFC 5272, *Certificate Management Over CMS (CMC)*

- RFC 5275, *CMS Symmetric Key Management and Distribution*

- RFC 5652, *Cryptographic Message Syntax (CMS)*

- RFC 5996, *Internet Key Exchange Protocol Version 2* IKEv2)

- RFC 6030, *Portable Symmetric Key Container (PSKC)*

- RFC 6031, *Cryptographic Message Syntax (CMS) Symmetric Key Package Content Type*

- RFC 6063, *Dynamic Symmetric Key Provisioning Protocol (DSKPP)*

- RFC 6160, *Algorithms for Cryptographic Message Syntax (CMS)*

---

[19] IPsec: Internet Protocol Security (secure network protocol suite); a summary is available in Part 1.

[20] IPsec IKE: Internet Key Exchange protocol (specified in RFC 7296 and later updates) used to set up a security association in the IPsec protocol suite.

[21] Kerberos: A network authentication protocol. See Part 3 for a summary.

[22] S/MIME: *Secure/Multipurpose Internet Mail Extensions (S/MIME)*.

[23] TLS: Transport Layer Security protocol as specified, for example, in RFC 5246 for version 1.2 and in RFC 8446 for version 1.3.

- RFC 6402, *Certificate Management Over CMS (CMC) Updates*

2.4 General Design Requirements for CKMS

Regardless of the key-management structure, any CKMS design **should** describe how it provides cryptographic keys to the entities that will use those keys to protect sensitive information. The CKMS design documentation **should** specify the use of each key type, where and how keys can be generated, how they can be protected in storage and during delivery, and the types of entities to whom they can be delivered. CKMS design is the subject of SP 800-130, *A Framework for Designing Cryptographic Key Management Systems*.

SP 800-152[24] contains requirements for the design, implementation, and procurement of a CKMS for the U.S. Federal Government, but it can be used as a model for other sectors. A key-management system can be designed to provide services for a single individual (e.g., in a personal data-storage system), an organization (e.g., in a secure Virtual Private Network (VPN) for intra-office communications), or a large complex of organizations (e.g., in secure communications for the U.S. Government). A CKMS can be owned or rented. However, regardless of the design or source for the key-management system, the recommendations of Part 1 and SP 800-152 **shall** be followed.

2.5 Trust

Because the compromise of a cryptographic key compromises all of the information and processes protected by that key, it is essential that client nodes be able to trust that keys and/or key components come from a trusted source, and that their confidentiality (if required) and integrity have been protected both in storage and in transit. In the case of secret keys, the exposure of a key by any member of a communicating group or on any link between any pair in that group compromises all of the information that was shared by the group using that key. As a result, it is important to avoid using a key from an unauthenticated source,[25] to protect all keys and key components in transit, and to protect stored keys for as long as any information protected under those keys requires protection. Cryptographic confidentiality and integrity mechanisms are most commonly used to establish trust anchors that enforce trust policies and practices. A *trust anchor* is an authoritative entity for which trust is assumed and not derived. For example, in a public key infrastructure (PKI), a trust anchor is an authoritative entity represented by a public key and associated data. "Trust anchor" also refers to the public key of this CA.

2.6 Revocation and Suspension

Section 8.3.5 of Part 1 discusses the revocation of cryptographic keys. Symmetric keys are often revoked by the use of Compromised Key Lists (CKLs). Certificate Revocation Lists (CRLs) are

---

[24] SP 800-152, *A Profile for U.S. Federal Cryptographic Key Management Systems*.

[25] For example, in TLS, unauthenticated clients send keys to servers. This is permitted where the server is only serving publicly-available information, and the TLS session is used to (1) assure the client of the integrity and source of the information and (2) protect the privacy of the client so that others cannot see what information the client has chosen to access. However, keys from unauthenticated clients should not be used to protect the information of entities other than the client or to authenticate the client to the server or other entities, as the trustworthiness of an unauthenticated client's keys is unclear.

commonly used to revoke public key certificates, thus revoking the private key corresponding to the public key in the certificate. Regardless of whether symmetric or asymmetric keys are used, a means of revoking keys is required. This Recommendation will use the term *revoked key notification* (RKN) to refer to a mechanism to revoke keys. An RKN may include the revocation reason and an indication of when the revocation was requested. The inclusion of the revocation reason can be useful in risk decisions regarding the information that was received or stored using those keys.

A key may also be suspended from use for a variety of reasons, such as an unknown status of the key or due to the key owner being temporarily unavailable (e.g., the key owner is on extended leave). In the case of a certificate suspension, the intent is to suspend the use of the public key included in the certificate (e.g., to not verify digital signatures or establish keys while the use of the certificate is suspended). This may be communicated to relying parties as an "on hold" revocation reason code in a CRL and in an Online Certificate Status Protocol (OCSP) response. The certificate may later be revoked (e.g., a compromise of the private key corresponding to the public key in the certificate was confirmed) or the certificate may be reactivated (e.g., the key has not been compromised or the owner returned to work). Section 7.3.5 of Part 1 discusses the suspended state for a key.

3   Key Management Planning

3.1   Background

Federal government organizations are required by statutory and administrative rules and guidelines to protect the confidentiality and integrity of their sensitive information and processes. Federal agencies are required to determine a FIPS 200[26] impact level (i.e., Low, Moderate or High) based on the security categories defined in FIPS 199.[27] The security categories are based on the potential impact on an organization if certain events occur that jeopardize the information and information systems needed by the organization to accomplish its assigned mission, protect its assets, fulfill its legal responsibilities, maintain its day-to-day functions, and protect individuals.

An organization also needs to define its security objectives for storing and/or communicating its sensitive information. These objectives may include the following:

- Providing confidentiality for stored and/or transmitted data,

- Source authentication for received data,

- Integrity protection for stored/transmitted data,

- Entity authentication, etc.

If cryptography is used to satisfy the requirement to protect an organization's sensitive information and processes, developers, integrators, and managers need to ensure that each cryptographic implementation satisfies all system security, compatibility, and interoperability requirements that are associated with the system into which it is being integrated.

Program managers who oversee the implementation of cryptography in federal systems are responsible for ensuring that the systems include all mechanisms, interfaces, policies, and procedures that are necessary to generate or otherwise establish, acquire, distribute, replace, account for, and protect key information that is required for system cryptographic operations in accordance with the recommendations presented in Part 1 and the policies and practices identified in this Part 2 document (SP 800-57).

The development of new cryptographic systems, including CKMS, **should** ideally be conducted following the processes described in SP 800-160.[28] However, in many cases, systems that rely on cryptographic protection are already being used. Where such systems are being augmented or otherwise modified, security planning is still required, but the SP 800-160 processes will need to be abridged or otherwise adapted because of legacy constraints. Federal government organizations must still select SP 800-53 security controls based on system design, operational characteristics, and FIPS 199 impact levels.

---

[26] FIPS 200, *Minimum Security Requirements for Federal Information and Information Systems.*

[27] FIPS 199, *Standards for Security Categorization of Federal Information and Information Systems.*

[28] SP 800-160 Volume 1, *Systems Security Engineering: Considerations for a Multidisciplinary Approach in the Engineering of Trustworthy Secure Systems.*

3.1.1 Select SP 800-53 Controls

Given both the impact levels for an organization's sensitive information that needs to be protected using cryptography and the organization's security objectives (see Section 3.1), SP 800-53 security controls **should** be reviewed for applicability to the system, and either the use of applicable controls must be verified, or compensating controls that obviate the use of specific SP 800-53 controls must be documented. Note that the SP 800-53 security controls are described at a high level in many cases, and they may need to be interpreted or tailored to system characteristics and operational conditions.

3.1.2 IT System Examination

Most organizations have their sensitive information in an electronic form, and some of that information may be available online. The environment of the system on which the information resides needs to be examined to identify any CKMS components and cryptographic products that are available to provide the required cryptographic protections to that information (e.g., cryptographic applications and modules).

In all cases, any cryptographic functions **shall** be performed using FIPS 140-validated cryptographic modules. If any required functionality is not available, the shortfall needs to be identified.

3.2 Key Management Planning

Using the information from Section 3.1, determine how to integrate key management. Key management is often an afterthought in the cryptographic development process (i.e., when incorporating cryptographic processes into applications and systems). As a result, cryptographic subsystems often fail to support the key management functionality and protocols that are necessary to provide adequate security. Recognition of these shortcomings often results in modifications that may impact operational efficiency more than would have been the case if key management planning began during the initial development of the system or application. All cryptographic development activities **should** involve key management planning and development of specifications by entities designated as responsible for the secure implementation of cryptography into an information system. Key management planning **should** begin during the initial conceptual/development stages of the cryptographic development lifecycle or during the initial discussion stages for the application of existing cryptographic mechanisms into information systems and networks. The specifications that result from the planning activities **shall** be consistent with NIST key management guidance (see Part 1 and SP 800-152).

All cryptographic purchasing plans, development activities, and application integration plans **should** involve key management planning. In the case of planning for the acquisition and use of existing cryptographic devices or software, key management planning **should** begin during the initial discussion stages for cryptographic applications or implementation efforts. The planning **should** be evolutionary in nature, changing as the cryptographic application and requirements change, and **should** be consistent with NIST key management guidance. Key Management Plans

should ensure that the key management products[29] and services[30] that are proposed for the cryptographic device, application or process are provided with adequate security, and are supportable and operationally suitable in accordance with the FIPS 140 security policy for any associated cryptographic module.

For the application of existing cryptographic products for which a Key Management Plan already exists, the existing plan **should** be reviewed in the context of the application's environment, and requirements **should** be amended as necessary. Such a review process **should** begin as soon as a cryptographic product is selected.

3.2.1 Key Management Planning Process

Organizational Key Management Plans document the capabilities that cryptographic applications require from the organization's CKMS(s) and are often incorporated as appendices in system security plans. The purpose of these Key Management Plans is to ensure that any lifecycle key management services are supportable by and available from the CKMS in a secure and timely manner. The planning process must account for both the availability of critical resources and for assurance requirements implied by the organization's critical mission functions.

Key management planning involves the following steps:

1. An appropriate key management architecture is selected based on the available cryptographic mechanisms (see Section 3.1.2) and objectives (see Section 3.1). Section 2.3 provides examples of architectures to be considered.

2. A Key Management Specification is developed for each cryptographic product to be used in the system (see Section 4). When developing a Key Management Specification for a cryptographic product, the unique key management products[31] and services[32] needed from the CKMS to support the operation of the cryptographic product must be defined. The specification of cryptographic mechanisms,[33] including key management functions,[34] **shall** consider the organization's resource limitations and procedural environment.

   For example, an organization that lacks physical protection facilities, adequate vetting of support personnel, and the procedures and resources required for managing controlled unclassified information might find it difficult to satisfy the policies and procedures required for cryptography that are generally required for the protection of controlled unclassified information. Before either approving or rejecting specifications required for controlled unclassified information, the organization **should** consider the resource and operational implications of the decision.

---

[29] Key management products: keys, certificates, and tokens for various purposes.

[30] Key management services: e.g., key agreement or key transport.

[31] Key management products: keys, certificates, CRLs, CKLs, tokens, etc.

[32] Key management services: The generation, establishment, distribution, destruction, revocation, and recovery of keys.

[33] Cryptographic mechanism: elements of a cryptographic application, process, module or device that provide a cryptographic services.

[34] Key management functions: establish keys, certificates and the information associated with them; accounting for all keys and certificates; key storage and recovery; revocation and replacement; and key destruction.

A contrasting example is that of an organization that must exchange information that is assigned a Moderate or High FIPS 199 impact level; Moderate and High impact levels require a cryptographic module validated at FIPS 140 Level 3 or higher. Specifying a FIPS 140 Level 1 cryptographic module could adversely affect the organization's ability to continue to engage in mission-critical processing and communications partnerships.

If a Key Management Plan already exists for an organization, the Key Management Specification needs to be in conformance with the CKMS Security Policy (see Section 5). The CKMS Practice Statement **should** support both the CKMS Security Policy and the Key Management Specification.

3. Based on the Key Management Plan, a CKMS Security Policy (CKMS SP) is developed that documents the decisions made in developing the Key Management Plan. A CKMS SP is a set of rules that are established to describe the goals, responsibilities, and overall requirements for the management of cryptographic keying material throughout the entire key lifecycle (see Section 5).

4. A CKMS may be operated by the organization owning the information to be protected, or may be operated by another organization (e.g., under contract). The organization operating the CKMS develops a CKMS Practice Statement (CKMS PS). A CKMS PS specifies how key management procedures and techniques are used to enforce the CKMS Security Policy (CKMS SP).

3.2.2 Key Management Planning Information Requirements

The level of key management planning detail required for cryptographic applications can be tailored, depending upon the scope and complexity of the application. If an organization's cryptographic support requirements are limited, for example, to e-mail security for a small number of employees, extensive planning documentation is neither feasible nor cost-effective (unless such security documentation is justified by a very high level of sensitivity associated with the organization's application). On the other hand, cryptographic security for a collection of networks that support thousands, or tens of thousands of users require the kind of extensive documentation described in Section 3.2.1 and in Appendix B. Regardless of the size and complexity of a cryptographic application, documentation of some basic key management characteristics and requirements is strongly recommended. Some basic information that needs to be documented for all applications is provided in the following subsections.

3.2.2.1 Key Management Products and Services Requirements

The key management planning documentation[35] **should** describe the keying material requirements for the key management products [36] and services [37] to be provided: the types, quantities, cryptoperiod (lifetime), algorithms, metadata types and any other additional information needed

---

[35] The Key Management Specification, the CKMS Security Policy and the CKMS Practice Statement as discussed in Sections 4, 5 and 6.

[36] Key management products: keys, certificates, CRLs, CKLs, tokens, etc.

[37] Key management services: The generation, establishment, distribution, destruction, revocation, and recovery of keys.

(e.g., domain parameters).[38] If additional keys, certificates or tokens are required, the key management planning documentation **should** describe a rough order of magnitude for the quantities required. If the keys or certificates already issued (or planned to be issued) by the CKMS are adequate for the device, application or process described in the Key Management Specification, then the Key Management Specification **should** so state. Otherwise, any new or additional key, certificate, or token features (e.g., new certificate extensions or formats) **should** be described.

The requirement information for key management products and services may be included in table format. The following information **should** be included in the key management planning documentation: [39]

- The types of key management products[40] and services[41];

- The quantity of key management products required for the services to be provided (e.g., the number of keys to be issued per device, application or process to be keyed);

- The algorithm(s) employed for each key management product used and service provided by a device, application or process;

- The key information format(s) (reference existing specifications, if applicable);

- The cryptoperiods to be enforced (may be a general recommendation or a recommendation specific to a service, key type, device, application, process or organization);

- PKI certificate classes (as applicable);

- Tokens or software modules to be used (as applicable);

- Dates when keying material is needed (plans for the distribution of the initial keys and the frequency of replacement of the keys);

- Provision for review or revision of replacement plans when the circumstances underlying replacement frequency change;

- The projected duration of the need (for devices, applications, processes or organizations);[42] and

- The title or identity of the anticipated keying material manager (as applicable).

The format for the description of the key management products and services generally references an existing key specification. If the format of the key information is not already specified

---

[38] For example, cryptographic applications using public key certificates (i.e., X.509 certificates) **should** describe the class of certificates as identified by the CA, and whether certificates and tokens already issued to subscribers will be used for the cryptographic application, or whether the cryptographic application will require additional certificates and tokens.

[39] Note that some of this material may be included by reference (e.g., a distribution of cryptography by the using organization's CKMS).

[40] Key management products: keys, certificates, and tokens for various purposes.

[41] Key management services: e.g., key agreement or key transport.

[42] This can affect the strength of the mechanism, affect when the system must be replaced, etc. It should be crosschecked with the projected duration of the need.

elsewhere, then the format and medium **should** be specified in the key management planning documentation.

3.2.2.2 Changes to Key Management Product Requirements and Transition Planning

Over time, the cryptanalytic capabilities and processing power available for performing cryptanalysis will eventually overtake the protection afforded by the implemented cryptographic algorithms. Most often, the cryptanalytic advances require a transition from a key size currently in use to a larger key size, but they can also result in the need to move from one algorithm to another. Examples include past requirements to transition from DES,[43] Triple DES[44] and SHA-1[45] to stronger algorithms, and the postulated need to transition from logarithmic and elliptic curve algorithms (e.g., RSA,[46] Diffie Hellman[47] and ECDSA[48]) to algorithms more resistant to quantum computing. Regardless of the basis for transition and whether the transition involves a larger key size or a new algorithm, it is important to begin planning for transition as soon as possible after becoming aware of the need. Changes to either algorithm or key size most often require changes to the code and protocols, not just to configuration settings for the current code and protocols. Frequently, firmware or hardware changes are required. This always takes longer and is more complicated than expected. The transition period is usually measured in decades; during the period between the advent of a practical cryptographic attack and the completion of a transition, all information protected by the vulnerable cryptography is subject to disclosure, alteration, or both.

3.2.2.3 Key Management Products and Services Ordering

For keys distributed from a CA or other key processing center rather than keys established at client nodes using automated key establishment techniques, a description of the procedures for ordering keying material within a specified CKMS is required. Details **should** be included that are sufficient to permit a determination of the requirements for long-term support by the CKMS.

3.2.2.4 Keying Material Distribution

For keys distributed from a CA or other key processing center rather than keys established at client nodes using automated key establishment techniques, key management planning documentation **should** describe the distribution method. The distribution information will normally include how the key management products are distributed (e.g., by courier or using key transport protocols), how they are protected during distribution (e.g., key wrapping) and how they are distributed (e.g., by courier or using key transport protocols), the physical form of the product (e.g., electronic, PROM,[49] disk, paper, etc.) and how they are identified during the distribution process.

---

[43] DES: the Data Encryption Standard specified in FIPS 46.

[44] Triple DES: the Triple Data Encryption Algorithm specified in SP 800-67.

[45] SHA-1: Secure hash Algorithm 1 specified in FIPS 180.

[46] RSA: the Rivest-Shamir-Adelman algorithm approved in FIPS 186 for digital signatures and in SP 800-56B for key establishment.

[47] Diffie-Hellman: the key-establishment algorithm approved in SP 800-56A.

[48] ECDSA: Elliptic Curve Digital Signature Algorithm approved in FIPS 186.

[49] PROM: Programmable Read-Only Memory.

3.2.2.5 Keying Material Storage

Key management planning documentation **should** address key information storage (e.g., the media used and the storage location, if appropriate) and the method for identifying the information during its storage life (e.g., by key name and date). The storage capacity capabilities for the key management products[50] **should** be included.

3.2.2.6 Access Control

Key management planning documentation **should** address how access to the cryptographic application will be authorized, controlled, and validated for the request, generation, handling, establishment, storage, and/or use of key management products and services. Any use of authentication mechanisms such as passwords, tokens, personal identification numbers (PINs), or biometrics **shall** be included (with their expiration dates, where applicable). For PKI cryptographic applications, access privileges based on roles and the use of tokens **shall** be described.

3.2.2.7 Accounting for Keys and Certificates

Key management planning documentation **must** include a description of the accounting methods used for the keys and certificates employed by the cryptographic application (i.e., the use of an inventory and audit logs).

When using cryptographic functions[51] that employ keys, it is imperative to maintain a record of all long-term keys[52] in use. Inventory management is concerned with establishing and maintaining records of the keys and/or certificates in use; assigning and tracking their owners or sponsors[53] (who/what are responsible for the keys and where they are located or how to contact them); monitoring key and certificate status (e.g., expiration dates and whether compromised), and reporting the status to the appropriate official for remedial action, when required (e.g., to replace the key and/or certificate).

The use of logs to support tracking the use of key management products and services, (including the generation/establishment, storage, use and/or destruction of key information) **should** be described. The use of appropriate access privileges to support the control of key management products and services used by the cryptographic device, application or process **should** also be described in addition to the directory capabilities used to support PKI cryptographic applications, if applicable. There **should** be an identification of the circumstances under which human and automated tracking actions are performed and where multi-party control and split knowledge procedures are required, if applicable. Note that some of this material may, under some circumstances, be included by reference (e.g., reference to Department of Defense (DoD) Cryptographic Material System (CMS) documentation where the keying material is distributed by a DoD CKMS).

3.2.2.8 Compromise Management and Recovery

Procedures for the restoration of protected communications and stored information content in the event of the compromise of a key **should** be described. The recovery process description **should**

---

[50] Key management products: keys, certificates, IVs, etc.

[51] Cryptographic functions: algorithms and modes of operation.

[52] Session and ephemeral keys would not be inventoried, but audit records may include information about their use.

[53] See Section 1.5 for the definitions of owners and sponsors.

include the methods for re-keying (i.e., replacing the key and/or certificate). The methods for revoking keys **should** be described in detail, including the methods for issuing new certificates with new keys.

3.2.2.9 Key Recovery

Key information that is in active memory or stored in normal operational storage may sometimes be lost or corrupted (e.g., from a system crash or power fluctuation); cryptographic keys used to protect archived data may be required when accessing that data (e.g., to decrypt the data). Key recovery is used to obtain currently unavailable key information by an authorized human entity.

Key recovery may be possible if the key information has been backed up or archived. Key information may be recovered from backups during the key's cryptoperiod or from archives if the information has been archived; archived keys need to be retained as long as the archived information needs to be retained.

Sections 8.2.2.1 and 8.3.1 of Part 1 list key types that may be suitable for backing up or archiving, respectively. Issues associated with key recovery and discussions about whether or not different types of cryptographic keying material need to be recoverable are provided in Appendix B of Part 1. The recovery and permissible use of a recovered key is discussed in Section 5.3.4 of Part 1 and depends on the key type, assigned use, its cryptoperiod and whether it has been compromised.

An assessment needs to be made regarding which key information needs to be preserved for possible recovery at a later time. The decision employing a key recovery capability **should** be made on a case-by-case basis. The factors involved in a decision for or against key recovery **should** be carefully assessed. The trade-offs are concerned with continuity of operations versus the risk of possibly exposing the key and the information it protects if control of the key is lost.

A key recovery process description **should** include a discussion of the generation, storage, and access of the long-term storage keys used for the protection of backed-up and archived key information. The process of transitioning from the current to future long-term storage keys **should** also be included.

3.2.2.10   CKMS Enhancement (optional)

The use of FIPS-140-validated cryptographic modules to perform cryptographic functions is required for federal agencies and highly encouraged for others. Such use may reduce some of the documentation requirements and facilitate both system integration and logistics support. It also encourages the feedback of locally specific requirements to the CKMS planning process. However, requirements may be identified that are currently not supported by the appropriate CKMS. If applicable, it would be useful to identify and address required improvements to the CKMS in order to achieve the needed functionality. This will assist in identifying requirements for current and/or planned capability increments for the CKMS. Even if a device, application or process can be fully supported by the current or planned CKMS, improvements to the CKMS **should** also be identified if they improve functionality or reduce workload without sacrificing security. The identified requirements can be analyzed for potential upgrades to the CKMS, based on available cost, schedule, and performance constraints.

4   Key Management Specification

A Key Management Specification is the document that describes the key management products[54] that may be required to operate a cryptographic device[55] or application. Where applicable, the Key Management Specification also describes key-management components[56] that are provided by a cryptographic device. The Key Management Specification documents the capabilities that the cryptographic application requires from key sources (e.g., the CKMS). Examples are described in Appendix A to this Recommendation. Key Management Specifications are generally produced by developers or (where developers have failed to provide adequate capabilities) by integrators.[57]

Organizations **shall** select cryptographic devices and applications with cryptographic functions,[58] key management products[59] and key management services[60] that conform to NIST standards to the maximum extent possible, and new cryptographic application development efforts **shall** comply with NIST key management recommendations. Accordingly, NIST criteria for the security, accuracy, and utility of key management products in electronic and physical forms **shall** be met (e.g., see FIPS 140, SP 800-53, and Part 1). The methods used in the design, evaluation, programming, generation, production, establishment, quality assurance, and inspection procedures for key management products and services **should** be structured to satisfy such criteria.

For cryptographic development efforts, a Cryptographic Key Management Specification and acquisition planning process **should** begin as soon as the candidate algorithm(s) and, if appropriate, keying material media and format have been identified. Key management considerations may affect algorithm choice, due to operational efficiency considerations for the anticipated applications. When using existing cryptographic mechanisms to provide a cryptographic service[61] for which no Key Management Specification exists, the planning and specification processes **should** begin during device and source selection, and continue through acquisition and installation.

Where the criteria for current or anticipated security, accuracy, and utility can be satisfied with any of the organization's existing suite of key management products and services, one of those products and services **should** be considered. Where the application of current key management products and services results in reduced security, accuracy, utility, or added cost to a cryptographic application, then an organization may initiate efforts to develop and implement other key management product and service types, variations, and, as necessary, production processes.

---

[54] Key management products: keys, certificates, tokens, etc.

[55] Cryptographic device: a physical device that performs a cryptographic function (e.g., encryption).

[56] Key management components: The software module applications and hardware security modules (HSMs) that are used to generate, establish, distribute, store, account for, suspend, revoke, or destroy cryptographic keys and metadata.

[57] Note that a significant part of the information required is available in the Security Policy associated with each cryptographic module validation.

[58] Cryptographic functions: algorithms and modes of operation.

[59] Key management products: e.g., keys and certificates.

[60] Key management services: The generation, establishment, distribution, destruction, revocation, and recovery of keys.

[61] E.g., encryption and decryption, or the generation and verification of digital signatures.

However, such efforts **should** conform as closely as possible to NIST's established key management recommendations.

Processes for purchasing cryptographic products [62] and services [63] **should** include plans and provisions for the acquisition of keying material from trusted sources, secure paths for the transport of keying material, and/or FIPS 140-compliant automated key establishment mechanisms[64] (see SP 800-56A, SP 800-56B and SP 800-71). Key management requirements **shall** be included in service agreements or contracts associated with cryptographically protected services.

For any cryptographic device or application employed by the federal government, there **should** be a specification of the keying material that the device or application requires, an identification of whether the keying material is internally or externally generated, a specification of keying material input/output interfaces, and a description of interfaces to any required validation process. Development of the specification **should** be initiated before any cryptographic procurement is initiated. Algorithms, key lengths, cryptoperiods, key sources, input/output interfaces (where applicable) and keying material access and handling requirements **should** also be specified. For devices using cryptographic modules that are validated under FIPS 140, most of these requirements are specified in the security policy posted with the validation information for each module.[65] Note that all cryptographic modules used by federal agencies **shall** be validated in accordance with FIPS 140. These specifications are required by system developers as well as by the managers of systems into which cryptographic mechanisms[66] are integrated. They are also required by program managers who are responsible for the security of system implementations.

The types of key management components[67] that are required for a specific cryptographic device or application and/or for suites of devices or applications used by organizations **shall** be conformant to NIST standards and guidelines, and new cryptographic device-development efforts **shall** comply with NIST key-management recommendations. Accordingly, NIST criteria for the security, accuracy, and use of key management products in electronic and physical forms **shall** be met. Where the criteria for security, accuracy, and usability can be satisfied with standard key management components (e.g., PKI for public key systems), the use of those compliant components is encouraged. Appendix C is a checklist that may be used to guide Key Management Specification activities.

---

[62] Cryptographic products: software, hardware and firmware that includes one or more cryptographic functions (i.e., algorithms and modes of operation).

[63] Cryptographic services: e.g., confidentiality, integrity, source authentication, etc.

[64] Automated key establishment mechanisms: e.g., key agreement and key transport.

[65] This is just for the cryptographic module; it does not consider a system approach; e.g., at some security levels, keys can be entered into and output from the cryptographic module in plaintext form (manually entered keys can be in plaintext at levels 1 and 2). However, applications that use the cryptographic module may require that the keys be entered or output in encrypted form or as key components.

[66] Cryptographic mechanisms: e.g., mechanisms that provide confidentiality, integrity, source authentication, etc.

[67] Key management components: The software module applications and hardware security modules (HSMs) that are used to generate, establish, distribute, store, account for, suspend, revoke, or destroy cryptographic keys and metadata.

4.1 Key Management Specification Content

The level of detail required for each element of a Key Management Specification can be tailored, depending upon the environment and complexity of the device or application for which a Key Management Specification is being written. A Key Management Specification **shall** contain a title page that includes the device identifier or application type, and the developer's or integrator's identifier. Unless the information is tightly controlled, a Key Management Specification **should not** contain proprietary or sensitive information.

4.2 Cryptographic Application

A description of the cryptographic application will provide a basis for the development of the rest of a Key Management Specification. Cryptographic application coverage **should** consist of a brief description of the cryptographic application or device. This includes the purpose or use of the cryptographic application or device, and whether it is a new cryptographic application or device, a modification of an existing cryptographic application or device, or an existing cryptographic application or device for which no Key Management Specification currently exists. A brief description of the cryptographic services[68] that the cryptographic application or device provides **should** be included. Information concerning long-term and potential interim key management support for the cryptographic application or device **should** be provided.

Cryptographic applications may employ symmetric key cryptography, public key cryptography, or both. Examples of symmetric key cryptographic applications include full disk encryption for confidentiality, and the use of message authentication codes for integrity protection. Examples of public key cryptographic applications include 1) integrity protection for electronic mail, internet address information, and internet routing information using digital signatures and 2) asymmetric key transport to protect the confidentiality of symmetric keys in transit (encrypting the symmetric keys using a public key). Examples of applications that use both symmetric and asymmetric cryptography are Transport Layer Security (TLS) (using encryption to protect the transfer of data and information) and the encryption of electronic mail (e.g., SMIMEA[69]), where symmetric key cryptography is used to protect the confidentiality of the information, and public key cryptography is used to protect the confidentiality of the symmetric keys.

4.3 Communications Environment

The Key Management Specification **shall** provide a brief description of the communications environment in which the cryptographic device or application is designed to operate. Some examples of communications environments include:

1. Data networks (e.g., intranet, Internet, VPN);

2. Wired communications (e.g., landline, dedicated or shared switching resources); and

---

[68] Cryptographic services: confidentiality, integrity authentication, source authentication, non-repudiation support, access control, and availability.

[69] SMIMEA: Secure Multipurpose Internet Mail Extension Certificate Association.

3. Wireless communications (e.g., cell phones).

The environment description **shall** include any anticipated access controls on communications resources, data sensitivity, privacy issues, etc.

4.4 Key Management Metadata Requirements

A key's metadata is the information associated with a particular key that is used by a CKMS to manage the key. SP 800-152 states that the system designer should select the metadata that is appropriate for a trusted association with a key based upon a number of factors, including the key type, the key lifecycle states, and the security policy of the CKMS. The metadata elements cited in SP 800-152 specify a key's important characteristics, its acceptable uses, and other information that is related to the key. Metadata elements relevant to the management and use of a key must be correctly associated with a key and consulted whenever a key is stored, retrieved, loaded into a cryptographic module, used to protect data (e.g., including other keys), exchanged with peer entities authorized to use the key, and when assuring that a key is correctly protected.

For example, asymmetric cryptographic applications using public-key certificates (e.g., X.509 certificates) should describe the types of certificates in the metadata. Some examples of metadata elements from Section 6.2.1 of SP 800-152 include:

1. The different keying material classes or types required, supported, and/or generated (e.g., for PKI: signature keys, key establishment keys, and authentication keys; for symmetric keys: key wrapping keys, key derivation keys and data encryption keys);

2. The key management algorithm(s) (the applicable **approved** algorithms, e.g., FF DH[70] and/or RSA[71]);

3. The keying material format(s) (reference any existing key specification, if known);

4. The set of acceptable certificate policies (if applicable); and

5. Any tokens to be used for entity authentication (i.e., for access authorization or key entry).

The description of the keying material format (item 3 above) may reference a key specification for an existing cryptographic device. If the format of the keying material is not already specified, then the format and medium **should** be specified in any Key Management Specification. See Section 6.2.1 of SP 800-152 for a list of metadata elements to be considered for a CKMS.

4.5 Keying Material Generation

A Key Management Specification **should** include a description of the requirements for the establishment of keying material for the cryptographic device or application for which the Key Management Specification is written. If the cryptographic device or application does not provide key establishment capabilities, an identification of the keying material and source or method that will be required from external sources **should** be provided.

---

[70] Finite field Diffie-Hellman; see SP 800-56A.
[71] See SP 800-56B.

4.6   Keying Material Distribution

When a device or application supports the automated establishment of keying material, a Key Management Specification **should** include a description of the distribution method(s) employed for the initial keying material used by the device or application. The distribution plan may describe how the keying material is distributed (e.g., manual, key loader device, etc.) and the form used (plaintext, wrapped, as key components with dual control and split knowledge required, etc.) In the case of a dependence on manual distribution, the dependence and any handling assumptions regarding keying material **should** be stated.

4.7   Key Information Storage

A Key Management Specification **should** address how the cryptographic device or application for which the Key Management Specification is being written stores and protects key information[72] including how long it is to be stored. The integrity of all key information **shall** be protected; the confidentiality of secret and private keys and secret metadata **shall** be protected. When stored outside a cryptographic module, the method of protection depends on the impact level associated with the data protected by a key (see SP 800-152, Sections 6.1.2 and 6.2.1):

- For High and Moderate impact-level data, the confidentiality and integrity of the key information **shall** be cryptographically protected.

- For Low impact-level data, the confidentiality and integrity of the key information **should**[73] be cryptographically protected.

When cryptographic protection is used, the security strength of the protection **shall** be selected in accordance with the impact level associated with the data protected by the key (see Section 2.2 of SP 800-152). The generation and management of the storage-protection keys **shall** be described, including the process of transitioning from the current to future storage keys.

A Key Management Specification **should** also indicate how the key information is identified during its storage life (e.g., using a Distinguished Name or key identifier). The storage capacity requirements for storing the key information **should** be included.

4.8   Access Control

A Key Management Specification **should** address how access to the cryptographic devices or applications are to be authorized, controlled, and validated to request, generate, handle, distribute, store, use and/or destroy keying material. Any use of authenticators, such as passwords, personal identification numbers (PINs) and hardware tokens, **should** be included. For example, in PKI cryptographic applications, role and identity-based authentication and authorization, and the use of any tokens **should** be described.

---

[72] Keying material and the associated metadata.

[73] SP 800-53 permits low-impact information that is not protected cryptographically to be protected by any other method that provides the required confidentiality and integrity protection.

4.9   Accounting and Auditing

When using cryptographic mechanisms employing keys, it is imperative to keep track of all non-ephemeral keys authorized for use by their owner entities (e.g., in a key or certificate inventory and in audit logs). In the case of symmetric keys, this includes the keys used for interaction between entities within an organization and the keys used between organizational entities and entities external to the organization. For asymmetric key pairs, this includes key pairs owned by organizational entities – those entities authorized to use the private key of the key pair and any certificates containing the public key of each key pair.

Any Key Management Specification **should** describe any device or application support for the accounting of keying material and any support for or outputs to logs used to support the tracking of keying material generation, distribution, storage, use and/or destruction. The use of appropriate authorization mechanisms to support the control of keying material that is used by the cryptographic application **should** also be described. All Key Management Specifications **shall** identify where human and automated keying material inventory management[74] and audit logging are required and, if applicable, where multiple parties are required to perform some operation.

A list of key types is provided in Section 5.1.1 of SP 800-57, Part 1. Examples of metadata elements to consider for association with keys are listed in SP 800-152 and Section 6.2.3 of Part 1. Metadata elements may be explicitly recorded with each key or certificate, may be explicitly recorded for groups of keys or certificates, may be implicitly known or a combination thereof.

A long-term key[75] **shall** be inventoried along with any information associated with it (e.g., domain parameters and metadata).

The generation, distribution, storage, use and/or destruction of all keys **shall** be logged.

Some particularly important metadata elements that need to be associated with inventoried keys and certificates are the following. Note that in the case of certificates, some of the information may be available in the certificate itself.

1. Common elements that **shall** be specified as required by all Key Management Specifications include:

    -   Type of key – e.g., private signature key, symmetric data encryption key

    -   Key format – e.g., TLS/SSL server certificate, TLS/SSL client certificate, code signing certificate, email certificate, ASN.1, and Tag-Length-Value (TLV) encoding for symmetric keys

    -   Key length – e.g., 2048 bits, 256 bits

    -   Algorithm with which the key is used – e.g., AES, ECDSA, RSA

---

[74] Inventory management is concerned with establishing and maintaining an inventory of keys and/or certificates; assigning and tracking their owners, representatives and sponsors (who/what they are and where they are located or how to contact them); automating the entry of keys and certificates into the inventory; installing keys and certificates into devices, if appropriate; monitoring key and certificate status (e.g., expiration dates and whether compromised), and reporting the status to the appropriate official for remedial action, when required.

[75] A key other than an ephemeral key or a key used for a single communication session.

- Schemes or modes of operation – e.g., digital signatures, DH, GCM, etc.
- Key source:
  - A description of where the key was generated and by what/whom
  - How the key was generated and distributed (e.g., using a DH key agreement scheme, generated by an RBG and transported using RSA OAEP)
  - The identifier of any keys used during the generation or distribution process (e.g., pointers to other keys in the inventory or database)
- Key owner(s)/authorized users/subject name:
  - Entity identifier(s)
  - Contact information for the owner or entity sponsor (e.g., email, phone)
- Application type(s) for the use of the key – e.g., email, file encryption, code signing
- Installed location information (as appropriate)
  - Address
  - Type of device on which it is installed
  - Location on device (e.g., ID, file path, account, etc.)
- Status – e.g., OK to use, compromised (with date), revoked (with date and reason), suspended (with start date and projected suspension end date), destroyed (with date), etc.

2. Common elements that **should** be specified as required by all Key Management Specifications include:

- Key identifier
- Business application name/id[76]
- Applicable regulations and policies[77]
- Authorities responsible for approving systems using cryptography for activation and operation.
- Storage protection when outside a cryptographic module:[78]
  - The algorithm(s) used to protect the integrity of the keying material and metadata and a pointer to the keying material used for the integrity protection

---

[76] Important to organizations in tracking sets of distinct keys that are all serving the same application.

[77] Allows for rapid identification of impacted keys if a regulation is changed to be more strict, for example.

[78] Depending on the algorithm used for storage protection, integrity and confidentiality protection may require either one or two distinct keys.

       o   If the key type is a secret or private key, the algorithm used to wrap the key and a pointer to the keying material used for key wrapping

3. Elements that **should** be included as being required for symmetric key systems:

- Cryptoperiods – by date or by usage:

  o   By date – start and end dates for the originator-usage period and recipient-usage period[79]

  o   By usage – current count and the usage-count limit for the originator-usage period

4. In the case of systems using asymmetric keys and PKI certificates (e.g., Transport Layer Security certificates), the following metadata elements **shall** be specified by all Key Management Specifications as being required:

- Certificate issuer – e.g., Issuer distinguished name

- Signature algorithm used to sign the certificate

- Subject type – indicating whether the certificate is for a CA or end entity

- Cryptoperiod[80] – start and end dates

- The corresponding key[81] – a pointer to the corresponding key

Also, in the case of asymmetric systems using PKI certificates (e.g., Transport Layer Security certificates), the following elements **should** be specified in Key Management Specifications as being required:

- Certificate serial number

- Authority Key Identifier

- Certificate Extensions

- Certificate validity period – start and expiration dates

5. In some other applications of public key cryptography (e.g., SSH), the following information **shall** be specified in Key Management Specifications as being required:

- Key subtype – e.g., Host private key, known host key, user private key, authorized key)[82]

- Account (to which the key is associated)

---

[79] See Section 5.3.5 of SP 800-57, Part 1.

[80] May span the validity periods of successive (i.e., replaced) certificates that include the same public key.

[81] If the key type is a private key, the corresponding key is the public key of the key pair; if the key type is a public key, the corresponding key is the private key of the key pair.

[82] Certificates and private keys are usually stored together. Because of the explicit trust model of SSH, public keys are stored separately. Consequently, it is important to know which component is where.

- Authorized key options (e.g., cert-authority, no-agent-forwarding, no-pty)[83]

4.10 Recovery from Compromise, Corruption, or Loss of Keying Material

A Key Management Specification **should** address any support for the restoration of protected communications in the event of the compromise, corruption, or loss of the keying material used by the cryptographic device or application. The recovery process description **should** include the methods for replacing keys and/or certificates with new keys. The methods for revocation and compromise notification (e.g., using RKNs) should be provided (e.g., the details for using Certificate Revocation Lists (CRLs) and Compromised Key Lists (CKLs)). When PKI certificates are used, a description of how certificates will be reissued with new public keys and replaced within the cryptographic application **should** also be included. General compromise-recovery guidance is provided in Section 9.3.4 of Part 1.

4.11 Key Recovery

Any Key Management Specification **should** include a description of product support or system functions for effecting key recovery. Key recovery addresses how unavailable keys can be recovered (e.g., encryption keys) from key backups or archives.

In the key-recovery process description, system developers **should** include a discussion of the generation, storage, and access to any keys used to protect the integrity or confidentiality of key information. Stored keys are expected to be protected as discussed in Section 5.7.

General contingency planning guidance is provided in Section 9.3 of Part 1. Key recovery is discussed in Appendix B of Part 1.

---

[83] These are critical to the reviewing the security of authorized keys, which grant access to systems and system-controlled functions.

5   CKMS Security Policy

An organization often creates and supports layered security policies, with high-level policies addressing the management of its information and lower-level policies specifying the rules for protecting the information.

- An organization's Information Management Policy governs the collection, processing, and use of an organization's information and should specify, at a high level, what information is to be collected or created, and how it is to be managed.

- The organization's Information Security Policy is created to support and enforce portions of the organization's Information Management Policy by specifying in more detail what information is to be protected from anticipated threats. and how that protection is to be attained. A Federal organization may have different Information Security Policies covering different applications of categories of information.

A CKMS Security Policy[84] (SP) is a high-level document that describes the authorization and protection objectives and constraints that apply to the generation, establishment, accounting, storage, use, and destruction of cryptographic keying material. It is intended to support an Information Security Policy by protecting the cryptographic keys and metadata used by a CKMS and to enforce restrictions associated with their use. A CKMS SP includes an identification of all cryptographic mechanisms and cryptographic protocols that can be used by the CKMS. A CKMS SP[85] also includes a set of rules that are established to describe the goals, responsibilities, and overall requirements for the management of cryptographic keying material throughout the entire key lifecycle, including when they are operational, stored, transported and used. As stated in SP 800-152, a CKMS SP **should** include the following:

a) The names of the organization(s) adopting the policy;

b) Who (person, title or role) is authorized to approve/modify the policy;

c) The impact-levels of the information that is specified in and controlled by the policy;

d) The primary data and key/metadata protection services (i.e., data confidentiality, data integrity, source authentication) that are to be provided by the CKMS;

e) The security services (e.g., personal accountability, personal privacy, availability, anonymity, unlinkability, unobservability) that can be supported by the CKMS;

f) Sensitivity and handling restrictions for keys and associated metadata;

g) The algorithms and all associated parameters to be used for each impact-level and with each protection service;

h) The expected maximum lifetime of keys and metadata for each cryptographic algorithm used;

---

[84] Note that in the original version of Part 2, the CKMS Security Policy was called a Key Management Policy (KMP). The name has been changed to be consistent with SP 800-152.

[85] In a purely PKI environment, the CKMS SP may be a Certificate Policy (CP) in conformance to RFC 3647, the Internet X.509 Public Key Infrastructure Certificate Policy and Certification Practices Framework.

i) The acceptable methods of user/role and source authentication for each information impact-level to be protected by a key and its associated metadata;

j) The backup, archiving and recovery requirements for keys and metadata at each information impact-level;

k) The roles to be supported by the CKMS,

l) The access control and physical security requirements for the CKMS's keys and metadata for each impact-level;

m) The means and rules for recovering keys and metadata; and

n) The communication protocols to be used when protecting sensitive data, keys, and metadata.

CKMS SPs are implemented through a combination of security mechanisms and procedures. An organization uses security mechanisms (e.g., safes, alarms, random number generators, encryption algorithms, signature, and authentication algorithms) as tools to implement a policy. However, key-management components will produce the desired results only if they are properly configured and maintained.

CKMS Security Policy statements are supported by CKMS Practice Statements (PS) that document the procedures that system administrators and users follow when establishing and maintaining key-management components [86] using the CKMS. CKMS Practice Statement requirements are described in Section 6 below. The procedures documented in the CKMS Practice Statement describe how the security requirements in the CKMS SP are met and are directly linked to the key-management components employed by an organization (see PKI 01).

U. S. Government agencies that use cryptography are responsible for defining the CKMS SP that governs the lifecycle for the cryptographic keys as specified in Section 6.3 of SP 800-152 and in Part 1, Sections 7 and 8. A CKMS Practice Statement is then developed, based on the CKMS SP and the actual applications supported.

Policy documentation requirements associated with small scale or single-system cryptographic applications will obviously not be as elaborate as those required for large and diverse government agencies that are supported by several information technology systems. However, any organization that employs cryptography to provide security services is likely to require some level of policy, practices and planning documentation.

5.1 Policy Content

The policy document or documents that comprise the CKMS SP include high-level key management structure and responsibilities, governing standards and guidelines, organizational dependencies and other relationships, and security objectives.

---

[86] Key management components: The software module applications and hardware security modules (HSMs) that are used to generate, establish, distribute, store, account for, suspend, revoke, or destroy cryptographic keys and metadata.

Most currently available guidance for CKMS SP development is focused primarily on the use of asymmetric algorithms and X.509 certificate-based key establishment and transport in a public key infrastructure (PKI) environment. In that environment, the CKMS SP is usually a stand-alone document known as a Certificate Policy (CP).[87] Certificate issuance organizations also publish CPs.[88] Although some interpretation is required,[89] most of the guidance herein applies to symmetric-key environments as well.

The scope of a CKMS SP may be limited to the management of certificates for a single PKI certification authority (CA) and its supporting components,[90] or to a symmetric-key environment[91] between peer entities or between subscribers and a key center in a single key-center environment. Alternatively, the scope of a CKMS SP may include certificate management in a hierarchical PKI, a meshed PKI, or multiple-center symmetric-key environments (see Section 2.3). Note that multiple CAs or symmetric-key environments may operate under a single CKMS SP.

The CKMS SP is used for several different purposes. The CKMS SP is used to guide the development of CKMS Practice Statements for each CA or symmetric key center or multiple-center group that operates under its provisions. CA managers from the PKIs of other organizations' PKIs may review the CKMS SP/CP before cross-certification, and managers of symmetric-key CKMS may review the CKMS SP before joining new or existing multiple-center groups. Auditors and accreditors will use the CKMS SP as the basis for their reviews of CA and/or symmetric-key CKMS operations. Application owners that are considering a PKI certificate source **should** review a CKMS SP/CP to determine whether its certificates are appropriate for their applications.

5.1.1 General Policy Content Requirements

Although detailed formats are specified for some environments (e.g., see Appendix A for a PKI CP format), the policy documents into which key-management information is inserted may vary from organization to organization. In general, the information **should** appear in top-level organizational information systems policies and practices documents. The policy need not always be elaborate. A degree of flexibility may be desirable with respect to actual organizational assignments and operations procedures in order to accommodate organizational and information infrastructure changes over time. However, the CKMS SP needs to establish a policy foundation for the full set of key management functions.

---

[87] Examples include *Department of the Treasury Public Key Infrastructure (PKI) X.509 Certificate* Policy (Treasury CP) *Reference Certificate* Policy (NISTIR 7924), and the *United States Department of Defense X.509 Certificate Policy* (DoD Cert Policy).

[88] For example, the *CertiPath X.509 Certificate Policy* (CP X509 CP).

[89] For example, the use of key-encrypting keys for key wrapping, compromised key lists rather than certificate revocation lists, and message authentication codes rather than digital signatures.

[90] This is generally the case when a single CA serves an enterprise, or a CA participates in a mesh (see Section 2.3.7). (PKI 01).

[91] Special Publication 800-71, DRAFT *Recommendation for Key Establishment Using Symmetric Block Ciphers*, National Institute of Standards and Technology, July 2016.

5.1.2 Security Objectives

A CKMS SP **should** state the security objectives that are applicable to and expected to be supported by the CKMS. The security objectives **should** include the identification of:

(a) The nature of the information to be protected (e.g., financial transactions, privacy-sensitive information, critical process data);

(b) The classes of threats against which protection is required (e.g., the unauthorized modification of data, the replay of communications, the fraudulent repudiation of transactions, the disclosure of information to unauthorized parties);

(c) The FIPS 199 impact level that is determined by the consequences of a compromise of the protected information and/or processes (including the sensitivity and perishability of the information);

(d) The cryptographic protection mechanisms to be employed (e.g., message authentication codes, digital signatures, encryption);

(e) The protection requirements for cryptographic processes and keying material (e.g., tamper-resistant processes, confidentiality of keying material); and

(f) Applicable statutes, and executive directives and guidance to which the CKMS and its supporting documentation **shall** conform.

The statement of security objectives will provide a basis and justification for other provisions of the CKMS SP.

5.1.3 Organizational Responsibilities

The CKMS SP **should** identify the required CKMS management responsibilities and roles, including organizational contact information. The following classes of organizational responsibilities **should** be identified:

(a) Identification of an Individual Having Ultimate Responsibility for Key Management Within the Organization (e.g., the keying material manager) – Since the security of all data that is cryptographically protected depends on the security of the cryptographic keys employed, the ultimate responsibility for key management **should** reside at the executive level. The individual responsible for keying material management functions **should** report directly to the organization's Chief Information Officer (CIO). [92] The individual responsible for keying material management **should** have capabilities and trustworthiness commensurate with the responsibility for maintaining the authority and integrity of all formal, electronic transactions and the confidentiality of all information that is sufficiently sensitive to warrant cryptographic protection.

(b) Identification of Infrastructure Entities and Roles - The CKMS SP **should** identify organizational responsibilities for critical CKMS roles. The following roles (where

---

[92] When an organization does not have a CIO position, FISMA requires the associated responsibilities to be handled by a comparable agency official.

applicable to the type and complexity of the infrastructure being established) **should** be assigned and their responsibilities specified:

- o Central Oversight Authority (may be the keying material manager),
- o Oversight for relationships with public key certification authorities (CAs) or symmetric key centers,
- o Oversight for relationships with registration authorities (RAs),
- o Compliance auditor (ensures compliance with regulations and internal controls, and
- o Oversight for operations (e.g., key processing facility (ies), service agents).

(c) Basis for and Identification of Essential Key Management Roles – The CKMS SP **should** also identify responsible organization(s), organization (not individual) contact information, and any relevant statutory or administrative requirements for the following functions, at a minimum:

- o System administration and operation;
- o Key generation or acquisition;
- o Agreements with partner organizations regarding the mutual acceptance of keying material, as appropriate (e.g., agreements associated with multiple-center groups);
- o Key establishment using manual or automated processes;
- o Establishment of cryptoperiods, validity periods, and/or originator/recipient usage periods;
- o Establishment of and accounting for keying material;
- o Protection of secret and private keys and related materials;
- o Emergency and routine revocation and suspension of keying material (e.g., revocation due to the compromise of a key);
- o Auditing key usage logs;
- o Key and/or certificate inventory management;
- o Destruction of revoked or expired keys;
- o Key back-up, archiving, and recovery;
- o Compromise recovery;
- o Contingency planning;
- o Disciplinary consequences for the willful or negligent mishandling of keying material; and
- o Generation, approval, and maintenance of key management policies and practice statements.

5.1.4   Sample CKMS SP Format

The sample format provided in this subsection is designed to be compatible with the standard format for PKI certificate policies (Appendix A). The sample format differs somewhat from that for PKI certificate policies (CPs) because some key management characteristics of and requirements for CKMS that accommodate symmetric keys differ from those for a purely PKI-based CKMS. The sample CKMS SP format below includes the general information called for in Subsections 5.1.2 and 5.1.3 above, plus some additional material that may be required in some administrative environments. As stated above, variations among organizational structures and needs will necessarily result in variations in the form and content of policy documentation. The sample CKMS SP format is provided as a general guide rather than as a mandatory template.

(a) *Introduction* -

The *Introduction* identifies and introduces the provisions of the policy document and indicates the security objectives and the types of entities and applications for which the CKMS SP is targeted. This section has the following subsections: 1) Overview, 2) Identification, 3) Community and Applicability, and 4) Contact Details.

Overview - This subsection introduces the CKMS SP.

Objectives – This subsection states the security objectives applicable to and expected to be supported by the CKMS. The *Objectives* subsection **should** include the elements of information called for in Section 5.1.2 (Security Objectives). (Note that in the case of a CP for a purely PKI environment, the *Overview* is followed by an *Identification* subsection that provides any applicable names or other identifiers, including ASN.1 object identifiers, for the set of policy provisions.)

Community and Applicability - This subsection identifies the types of entities that establish keys or distribute certificates. In the general case of the CKMS, this will include the responsible entities identified in the "Identification of Infrastructure Entities and Roles" element of Section 5.1.3 (Organizational Responsibilities). (Note that in the case of a CKMS that includes a PKI CA, this subsection **should** identify the types of entities that issue certificates or that are certified as subject CAs, the types of entities that perform RA functions, and the types of entities that are certified as subject end entities or subscribers.) This subsection may also contain:

- A list of applications for which the issued certificates and/or identified key types are suitable. (Examples of applications in this case are: electronic mail, retail transactions, contracts, travel orders, etc.)

- A list of applications to which the use of the issued certificates and/or identified key types is restricted. (This list implicitly prohibits all other uses for the certificates or key types.)

- A list of applications for which the use of the issued certificates and/or identified key types is prohibited.

Contact Details - This subsection includes the organization, telephone number, and mailing and/or network address of the keying material manager. This is the authority responsible for the registration, maintenance, and interpretation of the CKMS SP (see Section 4.1.3).

(b) *General Provisions* –

The *General Provisions* section of the CKMS SP identifies any applicable policies regarding a range of legal and general practices topics. This section may contain subsections covering 1) obligations, 2) liability, 3) financial responsibility, 4) interpretation and enforcement, 5) fees, 6) publication and repositories, 7) compliance auditing, 8) confidentiality, and 9) intellectual property rights. Each subsection may need to separately state the provisions applying to each CKMS entity type.[93] Note that many of the general provisions require input from and/or review by procurement elements of the organization.

Obligations - This subsection contains, for each entity type, any applicable policies regarding the entity's obligations to other entities. Such provisions may include: 1) keying material manager and/or Central Oversight Authority obligations, 2) key center obligations (symmetric key management-specific), 3) multiple-center group obligations (symmetric key management-specific) 4) service agent obligations, 5) CA and/or RA obligations (public key management-specific), 6) User obligations (including client nodes and public key subscribers and relying parties), 7) key-recovery agent obligations, and 8) keying material repository obligations.

Liability - This subsection contains, for each entity type, any applicable policies regarding the apportionment of liability (e.g., warranties and limitations on warranties, kinds of damages covered and disclaimers, loss limitations per certificate or per transaction, and other exclusions, e.g., acts of God).

Financial Responsibility - For key and/or certificate providers (e.g., key processing facilities, PKI CAs, key or certificate repositories, PKI RAs), this section contains any applicable policies regarding financial responsibilities, such as 1) an indemnification statement, 2) fiduciary relationships (or lack thereof) among the various entities, and 3) administrative processes (e.g., accounting, audit).

Interpretation and Enforcement - This subsection contains any applicable policies regarding the interpretation and enforcement of the CKMS SP or CKMS Practice Statement, addressing such topics as 1) governing law; 2) dispute resolution procedures; and 3) other technical contract issues, such as the severability of provisions, survival, merger, and notice.

Fees - This subsection contains any applicable policies regarding interagency reimbursement or fees charged by key and/or certificate providers (e.g., reimbursement for key-center management, certificate issuance or renewal fees, a certificate access fee, revocation or status information access fee, key recovery fee, reimbursement for information desk services, fees for other services such as policy information, refund policy).

Publication and Repositories - This subsection contains any applicable policies regarding 1) a key and/or certificate source's obligations, where keys are not locally generated, to publish information regarding its practices, its products (e.g., keys and/or certificates), and

---

[93] E.g., PKI CA, PKI repository, PKI RA, PKI subscriber, key recovery agent (KRA) and/or PKI relying party in public key management and central oversight authority, key centers, multiple-center groups, service agents, and client nodes in the case of symmetric key management.

the current status of such products; 2) the frequency of publication; 3) access control on published information (e.g., policies, practice statements, certificates, key and/or certificate status, RKNs); and 4) requirements pertaining to the use of repositories operated by private-sector CAs or by other independent parties.

Compliance Audit[94] - This subsection addresses any high-level policies regarding 1) the frequency of compliance audits for CKMS entities, 2) the identity/qualifications of the compliance auditor, 3) the auditor's relationship to the entity being audited, 4) topics covered under the compliance audit,[95] 5) actions taken as a result of a deficiency found during a compliance audit, and 6) the dissemination of compliance audit results.

Confidentiality Policy - This subsection states policies regarding 1) the types of information that **shall** be kept confidential by CKMS entities, 2) the types of information that are not considered confidential, 3) the dissemination of reasons for the revocation of certificates and symmetric keys, 4) the release of information to third parties (e.g., legal entities), 5) information that can be revealed as part of civil discovery (e.g., material that may be subject to FOIA[96] requests or subpoenas in civil actions), 6) the disclosure of keys or certificates by CKMS entities at subscriber/user request, and 7) any other circumstances under which confidential information may be disclosed.

Intellectual Property Rights - This subsection addresses policies concerning the ownership rights of certificates, practice/policy specifications, names, and keys.

(c) *Identification and Authentication* –

The *Identification and Authentication* section describes circumstances and identifies any applicable regulatory authority and guidelines regarding the authentication of a certificate applicant or key requestor[97] prior to the issuing of key(s) or certificate(s) by a keying material source. This section also includes policies regarding the authentication of parties requesting key or certificate replacement, key recovery or revocation. Where applicable, this section also addresses CKMS naming practices, including name ownership recognition and name dispute resolution. This section of the CKMS SP has the following subsections:

- Initial Registration,

- Routine Key and/or Certificate Replacement,

- Re-keying and Certificate Replacement After Revocation,

- Key Recovery, and

- Revocation Request.

---

[94] Note that a compliance auditor (who audits the procedures against the practice statements and policies) is different than an auditor that examines the information recorded by an operational system (e.g., key generation, key recovery, etc.).

[95] May be by reference to audit guidelines documents.

[96] FOIA: Freedom of Information Act.

[97] An entity that requests a new key for use; distinct from a key-recovery requestor.

(d) *Operational Requirements* –

The *Operational Requirements* section specifies policies regarding the imposition of requirements on CKMS entities with respect to various operational activities. This section should address the following topics, as appropriate:

- Request for actions needed to establish keys or certificates,
- Initial issuance of key and/or certificates,
- Validity checking and acceptance of keys and certificates,
- Establishing and maintaining inventories of keys and certificates that include expiration dates and linking keys to owner and sponsor identities,
- Notification to key owners when keys or certificates are about to expire,
- Key and/or certificate suspension and revocation,
- Security audit requirements,
- Key backup and archiving,
- Records archiving,
- Key and/or certificate replacement (i.e., re-keying and key derivation),
- Key recovery,
- Compromise and disaster recovery, and
- Key service termination (e.g., key center, CA, key storage).

Within each topic, separate consideration may need to be given to each type of CKMS component.[98]

(e) *Minimum Baseline Security Controls* –

This section states the policies regarding the management, operational, and technical security controls (e.g., physical, procedural, and personnel controls) used by CKMS components to securely perform 1) key generation, 2) entity/source authentication, 3) key establishment and/or certificate issuance, 4) key inventory creation and maintenance, 5) key and/or certificate revocation and suspension, 6) auditing, and 7) key storage and recovery (i.e., to and from backups and archives).

For federal government systems, based on the FIPS 199 impact level, the appropriate minimum baseline of security controls contained in SP 800-53 **shall** be implemented and described in this section of the CKMS SP.

(f) *Cryptographic Key, Message Interchange, and/or Certificate Formats* –

This section is used to state policies specifying conformance to specific standards and/or guidelines regarding 1) key management architectures and/or protocols, 2) key management message formats, 3) certificate formats and/or 4) RKN formats.

---

[98] The Central Oversight Authority, Key Processing facilities, Service Agents, Client Nodes, and Tokens.

(g) *Specification and Administration* –

This section of the policy document specifies:

- The organization(s) that has change-control responsibility for the CKMS SP,

- Publication and notification procedures for new CKMS SP versions, and

- CKMS Practice Statement approval procedures.

5.2 Policy Enforcement

In order to be effective, key management policies **shall** be enforced, and policy implementation **should** be evaluated on a regular basis and whenever there is a significant change in the cryptographic technologies used. Each organization will need to determine its enforcement requirements based on the sensitivity of information being exchanged or stored; the communications volume associated with sensitive or critical information and processes; the storage required for operational, backed-up and archived keys; provisions for key recovery; personnel resources; the size and complexity of the organization or organizations supported; the variety and numbers of cryptographic devices and applications; the types of cryptographic devices and applications; and the scale and complexity of protected communications facilities.

6   CKMS Practices Statement (CKMS PS)

The CKMS Practices Statement (CKMS PS) establishes a trust root for the CKMS and specifies how key management procedures and techniques are used to enforce the CKMS Security Policy (see Section 5) and to conform with the Key Management Specification (see Section 4). [99] For example, a CKMS Security policy might state that secret and private keys **shall** be protected from unauthorized disclosure. The corresponding CKMS PS might then state that secret and private keys **shall** be either cryptographically wrapped or physically protected, and that it is the responsibility of the network systems administrator to ensure that the keys are properly safeguarded. (The CKMS PS would also identify and provide contact information for the network systems administrator.) Note that the practices information contained in a CKMS PS is more prescriptive and specific than policy material contained in a CKMS Security Policy so it will be subject to more frequent change. Several CKMS PSs may implement a CKMS Security Policy for a single organization or one for each organizational key management domain (e.g., one for each of several CAs).

6.1   Alternative Practice Statement Formats

As in the case of the policy documentation, the security plan, practice document (i.e., CKMS PS), and/or procedure document into which a CKMS PS is inserted will vary from organization to organization. In general, the nature and complexity of the CKMS PS will vary with an organization's existing documentation requirements and the size and complexity of an organization's key management infrastructure.

Each CKMS PS applies to a single CKMS or a single domain of that CKMS. The CKMS PS may be considered the overall operations manual for the CKMS. Specific portions of the CKMS PS may be extracted to form application or role-specific documentation.[100] Auditors and accreditors may use the CKMS PS to supplement the CKMS Security Policy during reviews of CKMS operations.

6.1.1   Stand-Alone Practice Statement

While it is recommended that organizations create stand-alone practices documents (i.e., CKMS PSs), the practice information may be included in pre-existing top-level organizational information security policies and/or security procedures documents. A stand-alone CKMS PS may follow the general RFC 3647 format described for the CKMS Security Policy in Section 5.1.4, or it may follow a proprietary format. If the general outline of the sample CKMS Security Policy format is followed, the authors of the CKMS Security Policy will need to consider the basic differences in character between a CKMS Security Policy and a CKMS PS. While the CKMS Security Policy is a high-level document that describes a security policy for managing keys or certificates, the CKMS PS is a highly detailed document that describes how a CKMS implements a specific CKMS Security Policy. The CKMS PS identifies any CKMS Security Policies that it implements and specifies the mechanisms and procedures that are used to support each CKMS Security Policy.

---

[99] The term "CMKS PS" is used here to be consistent with SP 800-152. It is the same document formerly known as the Key Management Practice Statement (KMPS).

[100] E.g., a CKMS operations guide, a CA operations guide, a service agent manual, an operations manual for a key distribution or key translation center, a key storage and recovery manual, an RA manual, or a PKI user's guide.

Where the CKMS Security Policy specifies organizational roles and states requirements for mechanisms and procedures, the CKMS PS identifies more specific roles and responsibilities, and describes the mechanisms and procedures in detail. (Note that descriptive material can sometimes be included by reference to other procedures, guidelines, and/or standards documents.) The CKMS PS **should** include sufficient operational detail to demonstrate that the CKMS Security Policy can be satisfied by this combination of mechanisms and procedures.

6.1.2   Certification Practices Statement

A certification practices statement (CPS) is a PKI-specific document. In a purely PKI environment, the RFC 3647-specified CPS may serve as the CKMS PS for a CA. In such cases, the CPS will follow the RFC 3647 format summarized in Appendix A.

6.2   Common CKMS PS Content

Regardless of the CKMS PS format employed, the CKMS PS needs to include a minimum set of information. This subsection identifies the kinds of information that **should** be included in all CKMS PSs, when appropriate.

6.2.1   Association of CKMS PS with the CKMS Security Policy

The CKMS PS **should** identify the CKMS to which it applies and the CKMS Security Policy that its content implements.

6.2.2   Identification of Responsible Entities and Contact Information

The CKMS PS **should** identify the organizational entities that perform the various functions identified in the Organizational Responsibilities section (if following the organization of the CKMS Security Policy provided in Section 5.1.3). The individuals assigned to perform each key management role **should** be identified (e.g., by title). Contact information **should** include the individual's identity (e.g., a title), organization, business address, telephone number, and electronic mail address.

6.2.3   Key Generation and/or Certificate Issuance

The CKMS PS **should** prescribe key generation and/or certificate issuance functions. Key generation and/or certificate issuance **should** be accomplished in accordance with the guidelines contained in the key establishment sections of Part 1 (Section 8.1.5). The scope of key acquisition includes out-of-band procedures for acquiring initial and replacement keying material (e.g., initial key wrapping keys for communication with key centers and service agent procedures for the emergency replacement of compromised keys).

The CKMS PS generally identifies:

- Any management organization, roles, and responsibilities associated with key generation and/or certificate issuance,

- Any standards and guidelines governing key generation/certificate issuance facilities and processes, and

- Any documents required for authorization, implementation, and accounting functions.

For organizations that employ public-key cryptography, the CKMS PS (i.e., the CPS) **should** identify the certificate issuance elements of the CA (and its hardware, software, and human/organizational components as appropriate), as well as registration authorities (RAs).

Operating procedures and quality control procedures for key generation keying material and/or certificate issuance may appear either in the CKMS PS or in separate documents referenced by the CKMS PS. A documentation of the key generation and/or certificate issuance processes **should** also be included in order to establish a chain of evidence to support the establishment of the trusted source of keying material (e.g., a trust root for public key certificates or a symmetric key center).

6.2.4 Key Agreement

Key agreement involves participation by more than one entity in the creation of shared keying material. Public key techniques are normally employed to accomplish key agreement. See SP 800-175B and SP 800-56A for further discussions of key agreement techniques.

CKMS PSs may prescribe the organizational authority and procedures for authorizing and implementing key agreement between or among partner organizations. Within the context of a CKMS, key agreement will commonly be implemented by *client nodes*, using key agreement keys or key pairs received from *key processing facilities*.

6.2.5 Agreements Between Key Processing Centers

Organizations that have distinct public key certification hierarchies or meshes (see Section 2.3.8), but require secure communications between their domains may agree to cross-certify their organizations' CAs (i.e., key processing facilities). Similarly, in centralized symmetric key management structures, multiple key centers (i.e., key processing facilities) may agree to work together as a multiple-center group (see SP 800-71).[101]

Where entities within different organizations need to communicate securely with each other, the key processing facilities that serve them will need to establish formal agreements to work together to provide cryptographic services to their subscribers. For example, in PKI hierarchies or meshes, this would be a cross-certification agreement. CKMS PSs may prescribe the organizational authority and procedures for authorizing and implementing the cross-certification or sharing of keying material between or among partner organizations. Within the context of the CKMS, any authorization for these agreements **should** come from the Central Oversight Authority or its organizational equivalent. The cross-certification process between CAs or the sharing of keying material between key centers will normally be implemented in the key processing facility.

6.2.6 Key Establishment, Suspension and Revocation Structures

The CKMS PS **should** prescribe the organizational authority and procedures for the design and management of the organizational structure and information flow necessary to meet the

---

[101] These centers may establish formal agreements to share a common identity as a *multiple-center group*.

organization's key establishment, suspension,[102] and revocation[103] requirements. The CKMS PS **should** include or reference guidelines for maintaining the continuity of operations and maintaining both the assurance and integrity of the revocation and suspension processes. The CKMS PS **should** include guidelines for the maintenance of revocation lists[104] and the emergency replacement of keys and certificates as well as the timely and reliable routine establishment of keys and certificates. Both the establishment of an initial key between entities and changes to key establishment, suspension and revocation procedures **should** be authorized by the Central Oversight Authority and implemented by the key processing facility (or their equivalents) as described in the CKMS discussion (see Section 2.3.2). Additionally, a prescription of the audit and control of the key establishment process is necessary in order to maintain confidence in the integrity of the source of keying material.

6.2.7 Establishment of Cryptoperiods

The CKMS PS **should** prescribe cryptoperiods[105] for the keying material employed by an organization. Cryptoperiods **should** be approved by the Central Oversight Authority, or its organizational equivalent, and **should** be implemented by the CA or other key processing facility and client nodes (or their equivalents), as described in the CKMS discussion (see Section 2.3). Recommendations for establishing cryptoperiods are provided in Section 5.3 of Part 1.

6.2.8 Tracking of and Accounting for Keying Material

For keys distributed from a key processing center rather than established at client nodes using key agreement or other automated key establishment techniques, the CKMS PS **should** prescribe the organizational authority and procedures for the local creation of, distribution of, access to, and accounting for keying material required at each phase of the key management lifecycle (see Part 1, Sections 7 and 8). Any relevant accounting formats and database structures **should** be specified as required for:

- Keying material generation or recovery requests,

- Authorization of the distribution of specific keying material to specific organizational destinations for use in specific devices,

- Physical or automated establishment of keys or related key information (to include metadata),

---

[102] The validity of keys or certificates may be temporarily suspended for administrative or security reasons.

[103] Note that both public key certificates and symmetric keys may be revoked for a variety of reasons (administrative reasons, expiration of the key's assigned crypto period, or compromise).

[104] Including Compromised Key Lists for symmetric keys.

[105] If a key is retained indefinitely for operational use (e.g., for encryption, decryption, or signing), the probability that the key will become known through cryptanalysis, technical probing, malware, carelessness, or other methods increases over time. Depending on the criticality, volume, or perishability of the information being protected, longer or shorter operational lifetimes may be established for cryptographic keys. Some private-sector organizations neither change key variables and/or certificates nor make provision for users to change the keys and/or certificates. This is not recommended if the information has any privacy or security value. Ideally, an organization controls cryptoperiod determinations for the keys that protect its information.

- Key and/or certificate inventories,

- Receipts for keys or related key information,

- Reporting of the receipt of keys not accompanied by authorized transmittal information,

- Backup and archiving of key information,

- Requesting the recovery of backed up or archived key information, and

- The destruction of key information and related cryptographic materials.

General accountability recommendations are provided in Section 9.2 of Part 1; general key inventory guidance is provided in Section 9.5 of Part 1. Responsibilities and procedures **should** be identified for a CKMS, including the Central Oversight Authority, the CA or other key processing facility, service agent, and client node entities of the CKMS (or their equivalents).

6.2.9   Protection of Key Information

The CKMS PS **should** prescribe the responsibilities, facilities, and procedures for the protection of key information. This includes requirements for both the transmission and storage of key information. Requirements **should** be specified for a CKMS, including the Central Oversight Authority, CA or other key processing facility, service agent, and client node entities of the CKMS (or their equivalents). General recommendations for the protection of keys at different lifecycle stages (provided in Part 1, Sections 6.1.1, 7 and 8) **should** be included or referenced in the CKMS PS.

Note that where keys and key establishment security mechanisms are integral to a FIPS 140-compliant cryptographic module or application, reference to FIPS 140, its validated security level and any local physical security procedures may provide an adequate specification of protection practices.

6.2.10 Suspension and Revocation of Keying Material

The CKMS PS **should** prescribe the roles, responsibilities, and procedures for the suspension, and emergency[106] and routine[107] revocation of keying material. The CKMS PS **should** also prescribe the roles, procedures, and protocols employed at the key processing facility for the generation of RKNs for lost or destroyed certificates and keys, or for compromised certificates and keys.

The CKMS PS **should** also specify the roles, procedures, and protocols employed by service agent and client node entities, or their organizational equivalents, for the timely and secure reporting of potential compromises. The CKMS PS **should** identify the key types and reasons for which suspension and revocation actions are taken (e.g., suspension: key owner is on leave or a key compromise is suspected; revocation: key compromise or the key owner has left the organization); suspension and revocation are not necessary for ephemeral keys. General recommendations for

---

[106] An example of emergency revocation is revocation due to the known or suspected compromise of a key or key processing center.

[107] An example of routine revocation is revocation due to the key's owner no longer being authorized to use the key (e.g., the owner has left the organization).

key revocation are provided in Part 1, Section 8.3.5 and **should** be included or referenced in the CKMS PS.

6.2.11 Auditing

The CKMS PS **should** prescribe the roles, responsibilities, facilities, and procedures for the routine auditing of keying material and related records (e.g., metadata), including their generation, access and destruction. The CKMS PS **should** also describe audit reporting requirements and procedures. Auditing **should** occur wherever keys are handled (generated, stored, recovered, or destroyed).

Note that audit requirements will depend on the sensitivity of the information (including what is to be audited, the frequency of audits, and the frequency of reviews of different elements of the audit log). Note that audits will generally be conducted in facilities that distribute or receive keys (e.g., CAs or other key processing centers) rather than for cryptographic devices that use automatically established keys. However, developers **should** include logging and auditing capabilities in clients.

Conditions and procedures **should** also be included for unscheduled audits that are triggered by the observed and/or suspected unauthorized access, production, loss, or compromise of key information General audit recommendations are provided in Part 1, Section 9.2 and SP 800-152, Section 8.2.4.

6.2.12 Key Destruction

The CKMS PS **should** prescribe the roles, responsibilities, facilities, and procedures for any routine destruction of revoked or expired keys required at all CKMS elements. Key destruction conditions and procedures may also be included. Part 1 (Sections 8.3.4 and 8.4) and SP 800-152 (Section 6.4.9) include recommendations that **should** be included or referenced in the CKMS PS. Note that the destruction of keys is not completed until all copies are destroyed (including backups). Keying material in archives may need to be retained for later retrieval, but the keys **should** be destroyed when no longer needed.

6.2.13 Key Backup, Archiving and Recovery

OMB Guidance to Federal Agencies on Data Availability and Encryption, 26 November 2001, states that agencies **must** address information availability and assurance requirements through appropriate data recovery mechanisms such as cryptographic key recovery. For each CKMS, the CKMS PS **should** prescribe any roles, responsibilities, facilities, and procedures necessary for all organizational elements to backup, archive and recover critical key information, with the necessary integrity mechanisms successfully verified for the stored information, in the event of the loss or expiration of the operational copy of cryptographic keys under which the data is protected. Backups support recovering the current operational keys. Archives support the recovery of keys, primarily for the recovery of information after the key's cryptoperiod has expired. Key backup, archive and recovery are normally the responsibility of the Central Oversight Authority, or its organizational equivalent, although mechanisms to support recovery may be included in other components of a CKMS. Part 1, Appendix B.5, contains general key recovery recommendations that **should** be included in or referenced by the CKMPS. Examples of key recovery policies include the *Key Recovery Policy for The Department of the Treasury Public Key Infrastructure (PKI)*,

Federal Public Key Infrastructure Key Recovery Policy, and *Key Recovery Policy for External Certification Authorities.*

6.2.14 Compromise Recovery

For all CKMS elements, the CKMS PS **should** prescribe any roles, responsibilities, facilities, and procedures required for recovery from the compromise of a cryptographic key at any phase in its lifecycle. Compromise recovery includes 1) the timely and secure notification of owners and sponsors of compromised keys that the compromise has occurred and 2) the timely and secure replacement of the compromised keys. Emergency key revocation and the generation and processing of RKNs are elements of compromise recovery, but compromise recovery also includes:

- The recognition and reporting of the compromise,

- The identification and/or establishment of replacement keys and/or certificates,

- Recording the compromise and compromise recovery actions (may use existing audit mechanisms and procedures), and

- The destruction and/or de-registration of compromised keys, as appropriate.

Part 1 (Sections 9.3.4 and 10.2.9) and SP 800-152 (Section 6.8) contain recommendations regarding compromise recovery that **should** be included in or referenced by the CKMS PS.

6.2.15 Policy Violation Consequences

The CKMS PS **should** prescribe any roles, responsibilities, and procedures required for establishing and carrying out disciplinary consequences for the willful or negligent mishandling of key information. The consequences **should** be commensurate with the potential harm that can result from the violation of the organization's policy, its mission, and/or other affected organizations. While the procedures apply to all CKMS elements, the responsibility for establishing and enforcing the procedures rests at the Central Oversight Authority or its organizational equivalent. Consequences prescribed in a CKMS PS **shall** be enforced if they are to be effective. Note that it is necessary to correlate compromise records and the associated audit logs to the disciplinary actions that are taken as a result of violations of policies or procedures.

6.2.16 Documentation

The CKMS PS **should** prescribe any roles, responsibilities, and procedures required for the generation, approval, and maintenance of the CKMS PS. The generation and maintenance of CKMS PSs should normally be the responsibilities of the entity responsible for management of the CA/key center. The CKMS PS **should** be approved by the Central Oversight Authority or its organizational equivalent. The generation and maintenance of audit records are also normally the responsibilities of the Central Oversight Authority or its organizational equivalent. The generation and maintenance of registration, de-registration, revocation and compromise lists, revoked key notifications, and accounting documentation **should** be accomplished at the key processing facility(ies), service agent(s), and client nodes (or their organizational equivalents), as required by the CKMS PS (see Section 2).

Appendix A—CKMS Examples

This appendix contains examples of CKMSs: a PKI used for the distribution of asymmetric key pairs and two classes of key centers used for the establishment of symmetric keys.

A.1 Public Key Infrastructure (PKI)

One form of a CKMS is that of a public-key infrastructure (PKI) (shown in Figure 4). Comparing the PKI components against the CKMS components in Figure 1, the PKI's certification authority (CA) is the CKMS's key processing facility, and the PKI's registration authority (RA) is the CKMS service agent.

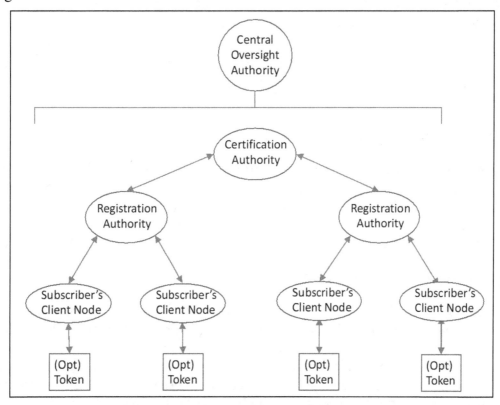

Figure 4: PKI Components

A.1.1 Central Oversight Authority

In a PKI, the Central Oversight Authority may be called a policy management authority or just a policy authority.

A.1.2 Certification Authority (CA)

The PKI Certification Authority (CA), is a central element of a key management facility.[108] The CA may create, sign, publish and manage public key certificates. Depending on the CA design, the CA may also generate asymmetric key pairs (e.g., for key establishment). See SP 800-15[109] and *X.509 Certificate Policy for the Federal Bridge Certification Authority (FBCA)* for more information about the responsibilities of a CA.

A.1.3 Registration Authority (RA)

A PKI's registration authority (RA) is an entity that enters into an agreement with a CA to collect and verify the identity of prospective subscriber entities and entity sponsors for the CA's services and other information that will be included in the subscriber's certificates. RAs register subscriber entities and sponsors, approve certificate issuance, and may perform key recovery operations. Not all RAs are authorized to perform all RA functions. An RA designated to perform key recovery operations may be referred to as a key recovery agent (KRA).

A.1.4 Subscriber's Client Node and Token

In this example, only human entities receive certificates as subscribers. Subscribers interface with the PKI and with others (called relying parties) using their client nodes. A subscriber's name appears as the subject of a certificate. If tokens are used, they are associated with a particular subscriber. Typically, either the client node or the subscriber's token contains the keying material to be used by the subscriber.

A.1.5 PKI Hierarchical Structures and Meshes

A hierarchical PKI is one in which all of the end entities and relying parties use a single "root CA" as their trust anchor. If the hierarchy has multiple levels, the root CA certifies the public keys of intermediate CAs (also known as subordinate CAs). These CAs then certify end entities' (subscribers') public keys or may, in a large PKI, certify other CAs. In this architecture, certificates are issued in only one direction, and a CA never certifies another CA that is "superior" to itself. Typically, only one superior CA certifies each CA. Certification path building in a hierarchical PKI is a straightforward process that simply requires the relying party to successively retrieve issuer certificates until a certificate that was issued by the trust anchor is located.

A widely used variation on the single-rooted hierarchical PKI is the inclusion of multiple CAs as trust anchors. In this case, certificates for end entities are validated using the same approach as with any hierarchical PKI. The difference is that a certificate will be accepted if it can be verified back to any of the set of trust anchors.

In a typical mesh style PKI (see Section 2.3.8); each end entity trusts the CA that issued its own certificate(s). Thus, there is no "root CA" for the entire PKI. The CAs in this environment have

---

[108] Note that a single CA may not comprise a complete key management facility. Depending on the architecture, other PKI key management functions include root CA, sub-CA, Registration Authority (RA), and Online Certificate Status Protocol (OCSP) response).

[109] SP 800-15, *MISPC Minimum Interoperability Specification for PKI Components.*

peer relationships; they are neither superior nor subordinate to one another. In a mesh, cross-certification between peer CAs may go in both directions.

A.2 Key Centers

Key Centers are often used in environments using symmetric keys. Two example architectures are that of a key distribution center and a key translation center (see SP 800-71).

A.2.1 Key Distribution Center (KDC) Architecture

A key distribution center (KDC) generates keying material as needed, either in response to a request or as determined by policy. Figure 5 shows a typical KDC architecture. KDCs are further described in SP 800-71.

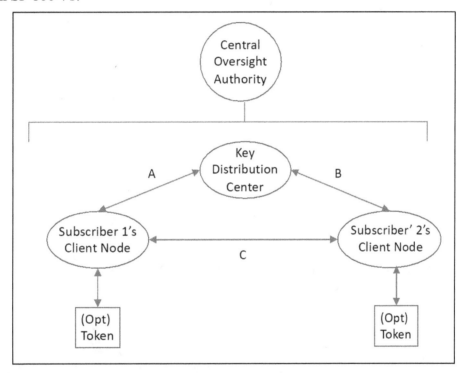

Figure 5: KDC Components

A.2.1.1 Key Distribution Center (KDC)

A KDC generates keys, either upon request or of its own volition, and distributes them to one or more of its subscribers. KDCs usually generate only symmetric keys. Subscribers share a key-wrapping key with the KDC that is used to protect the generated keys during communication. The KDC will use cryptographic techniques to authenticate requesting users and their authorization to request keys. Kerberos is a real-world example of a KDC.

A key generated by a KDC may be sent directly to one or more subscribers (using paths A and B in Figure 5) or multiple keys may be sent to one subscriber (e.g., Subscriber 1) who forwards them to another subscriber (e.g., using path A, followed by path C).

A.2.1.2 Subscriber Client Node and Token

Subscribers may request keys from a KDC (e.g., Subscriber 1 uses path A) only for their own use or may request keys to be shared with other KDC subscribers (Subscriber 2 in the figure). Alternatively, a KDC may voluntarily generate and distribute keys to its subscribers, either to be shared among two or more subscribers or to be used solely by a single subscriber. These keys may be stored by the client node or on the subscriber's token (if used).

A.2.2 Key Translation Center (KTC) Architecture

A KTC is used to translate keys for future communications between KTC subscribers. The architecture is shown in Figure 6 and is similar to the KDC architecture shown in Figure 5, except that a KTC is used instead of a KDC. Subscribers share a key-wrapping key with the KTC that is used to protect the generated keys during communication. KTCs are further described in SP 800-71.

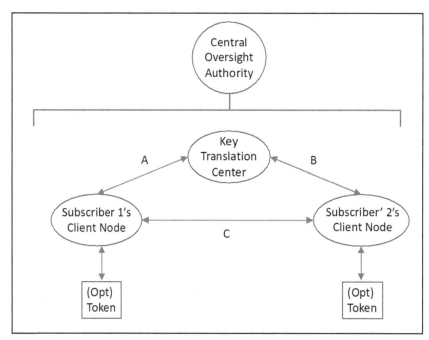

Figure 6: KTC Components

A.2.2.1 Key Translation Center (KTC)

When a KTC subscriber (e.g., Subscriber 1) needs to securely communicate with one or more other KTC subscribers (e.g., Subscriber 2) but does not share a key with them, then Subscriber 1 may generate keying material, wrap it using a key-wrapping key (KWK) shared with the KTC and send the wrapped keying material (using path A) to the KTC for "translation" into a form that can be understood by the other subscriber(s) (e.g., Subscriber 2). Depending on how the architecture is implemented, the translated keys may be returned to Subscriber 1 for forwarding to the other intended subscriber(s) (using path A, followed by path C) or may be sent directly to the other intended parties (using path B).

A.2.2.2 Subscriber Client Node and Token

Subscribers (e.g., Subscriber 1 in the figure)with a key generation capability may request key translation from a KTC (e.g., using path A) to be sent to other subscribers. These keys may be stored by the client node or on the subscriber's token (if used).

Appendix B—Key Management Inserts for Security Plan Templates

This appendix identifies a system security plan template and key management material that **should** be included in system security plans. The template information has been extracted from SP 800-18.[110]

Note that the following sample has been provided only as one example; this example is for a PKI. Organizations may use other formats and choose to update those to reflect any existing omissions based on this guidance. This is not a mandatory format; it is recognized that numerous agencies and information security service providers may have developed and implemented various approaches for information system security plan development and presentation to suit their own needs for flexibility.

Although the information identified in the key management appendix outline described at item 16 below may be distributed among other template elements rather than in a separate appendix, all of the information described in the key management appendix **shall** be included in the security plan for systems that employ cryptography.

1. Information System Name/Title

- The unique identifier and name given to the system.

2. Information System Categorization

- An identification of the appropriate FIPS 199 categorization (i.e., Low, Moderate or High).

3. Information System Owner

- The name, title, agency, address, email address, and phone number of the person who owns the system.

4. Authorizing Official

- The name, title, agency, address, email address, and phone number of the senior management official designated as the authorizing official.

5. Other Designated Contacts

- A list of other critical personnel, if applicable; include their title, address, email address, and phone number.

6. Assignment of Security Responsibility

- The name, title, address, email address, and phone number of the person who is responsible for the security of the system.

7. Information System Operational Status

- An indication of the operational status of the system. If more than one status is selected, list which status is assigned to each part of the system.

8. Information System Type

- An indication of whether the system is a major application or a general support system.

---

[110] SP 800-18 Revision 1, *Guide for Developing Security Plans for Federal Information Systems.*

9. General System Description/Purpose

- A description of the function or purpose of the system and the information processes.

10. System Environment

- A general description of the technical system, including the primary hardware, software, and communications equipment.

- Key management-specific information that needs to be included in this section, including the identification of any cryptographic mechanisms[111] employed (including key sources) and the location of any keys stored for future use as well as backed-up and archived cryptographic keys.

11. System Interconnections/Information Sharing

- A list of interconnected systems and system identifiers (if appropriate); provide the system, name, organization and system type (e.g., major application or general support system); indicate if there is an ISA/MOU/MOA on file, the date of any agreement to interconnect, the FIPS 199 category, the certification and accreditation status, and the name of the authorizing official.

12. Related Laws/Regulations/Policies

- A list of any laws or regulations that establish specific requirements for the confidentiality, integrity, or availability of the data in the system.

13. Minimum Security Controls

- A thorough description of how the SP 800-53 controls in the applicable Low, Moderate or High baseline are being implemented or planned to be implemented. The controls **should** be described by control family and indicate whether it is a system control, hybrid control, common control, scoping guidance is applied, or a compensating control is being used.

- Key management-specific information, including key inventory, backup, archiving, and recovery procedures in support of the recovery of encrypted files; controls for the verification of digital signatures and other integrity keying materials (e.g., certification authority and controls for determining completeness/correctness); key management procedures for key establishment (including key generation and distribution), storage, and destruction; and applicable cryptographic standards and guidelines for all cryptographic mechanisms employed. This information may be included in a key management appendix.

14. Information System Security Plan Completion Date

- The completion date of the plan.

15. Information System Security Plan Approval Date

- The date that the system security plan was approved and an indication of whether the approval documentation is attached or on file.

---

[111] Mechanisms to provide a cryptographic service, such as confidentiality, integrity or entity authentication.

16. Key Management Appendix

- **The Identification of the Keying Material Manager**: The keying material manager **should** report directly to the organization's chief executive officer, chief operations executive, or chief information systems officer. The keying material manager is a critical employee who **should** have capabilities and trustworthiness commensurate with its responsibility for maintaining the authority and integrity of all formal electronic transactions and the confidentiality of all information that is sufficiently sensitive to warrant cryptographic protection.

- **The Identification of the Management Entity(ies) Responsible for Certification Authority (CA) and Registration Authority (RA) Functions and Interactions:** Where public key cryptography is employed, either the keying material manager or his/her immediate superior **should** be designated as the organization's manager responsible for CA and RA functions. This section **shall** include references to any cloud computing or other shared services employed.

- **The Identification of the Management Entity (ies) Responsible for Symmetric Key Center Functions and Interactions:**

  Where a symmetric key center is employed, either the keying material manager or his/her immediate superior **should** be designated as the organization's manager responsible key center functions. This section **shall** include references to any cloud computing or other shared services employed

- **Key Management Organization:** The identification of job titles, roles, and/or individuals responsible for the following functions:

  a. Key generation or acquisition;

  b. Agreements with partner organizations regarding the cross-certification of any PKI keying material or sharing of keying material between symmetric key centers;

  c. Key establishment and revocation structure design and management;

  d. Establishment of cryptoperiods;

  e. Establishment of inventory management and accounting for keying material;

  f. Protection of secret and private keys and related materials;

  g. Emergency and routine revocation of keying material;

  h. Replacement of keys and/or certificates;

  i. Auditing of keying material and related records;

  j. Destruction of revoked or expired keys;

  j. Key recovery;

  k. Compromise recovery;

  l. Contingency planning;

  m. Disciplinary consequences for the willful or negligent mishandling of keying material; and

    n. Generation, approval, and maintenance of key management practices statements.

- **Key Management Structure:** As appropriate, a description of the management responsibilities for establishing cryptoperiods, key establishment, key certification, distribution, suspension, revocation, and any other procedures for encryption, signature, and other cryptographic processes implemented within the organization.

- **Key Management Procedures** (when appropriate)

    a. **Key Establishment:** Where applicable, a brief description of the procedures to be followed for key establishment of the initial key(s) and lower-level/replacement keys. This section includes references to applicable standards and guidelines. Some procedures may be presented by reference. Note that some organizations that employ cryptography may not generate keying material.

    b. **Key Acquisition:** An identification of the source(s) of keying material. A description of the ordering procedures (if appropriate) and examples of any forms employed in ordering keying material (e.g., by online request or paper request).

    c. **Cross-Certification Agreements** (applicable only to PKIs): A description of the cross-certification procedures and examples of any forms employed in establishing and/or implementing cross-certification agreements.

    d. **Agreements with Symmetric Key Partner Organizations** (applicable only to key establishment using symmetric-key algorithms): A description of the procedures and examples of any forms involved in establishing agreements regarding the mutual acceptance of keying material associated with multiple-center groups, as appropriate.

    e. **Distribution of and Accounting for Keying Material:** A description of the procedures for requesting keying material (either manual or online requests), including any forms associated with the request, the acknowledgement and disposition of the requests, the receipting for keying material, creating and maintaining keying material inventories, reporting the destruction of keying material, and reporting the acquisition or loss of keying material under exceptional circumstances.

    f. **Emergency and Routine Revocation of Keying Material:** A description of the rules and procedures for the revocation of keying material under both routine and exceptional circumstances, such as a notice of unauthorized access to operational keying material (i.e., a key compromise).

    g. **Protection of Secret and Private Keys and Related Materials:** The methods and procedures employed to protect keying material under various circumstances, such as during the pre-operational, operational, and revoked phase of a key's lifecycle.

    h. **Destruction of Revoked or Expired Keys:** The procedures and guidelines for identifying the circumstances, responsibilities, and methods for the destruction of keying material.

i. **Auditing of Keying Material and Related Records:** A description of the circumstances, responsibilities, and methods for the auditing of keying material records and monitoring key and/or certificate inventories.

j. **Key Recovery:** Specification of the circumstances and process for authorizing key recovery and an identification of the guidelines and procedures for key recovery operations.

k. **Compromise Recovery:** The procedures for recovering from the exposure of sensitive keying material to unauthorized entities.

k. **Disciplinary Actions**: A specification of the consequences for willful or negligent mishandling of keying material.

l. **Change Procedures:** A specification of the procedures for effecting changes to key management planning documentation.

Appendix C—Key Management Specification Checklist for Cryptographic Product Development

The following key management-related information for cryptographic product development may be useful to determine and resolve potential impacts to the key management infrastructure or other keying material acquisition processes in a time frame that meets user requirements. Yes/no responses **should** be provided to the following questions as well as additional information for each "yes" response. To the extent practical, SP 800-160,[112] **should** be followed in the development of cryptographic products.

1. Are unique key management products[113] and services[114] required by the cryptographic product for proper operation?

2. Are there any cryptographic capabilities to be supported by a CKMS that are not fully configurable in the cryptographic product?

3. Does the cryptographic module implement a software download capability for importing updated cryptographic functions?[115]

4. Does the cryptographic module use any non-keying material CKMS products or services (such as CKL/CRLs, seed key[116] conversion, etc.)?

5. Does the cryptographic module design preclude the use of any **approved** cryptographic algorithm?

---

[112] SP 800-160 Volume 1, *Systems Security Engineering: Considerations for a Multidisciplinary Approach in the Engineering of Trustworthy Secure Systems.*

[113] Key management products: e.g., keys, certificates, tokens, etc.

[114] Key management services: The generation, establishment, distribution, destruction, revocation, and recovery of keys.

[115] Cryptographic functions: algorithms and modes of operation.

[116] Seed key: The initial key used to start an updating or key-generation process.

Appendix D—References

The following publications are provided for reference. The provided publication dates refer to the last available version of the document as of the publication of this revision of SP 800-57 Part 2. When later revisions of these referenced documents are available, those versions should be referenced instead.

	Evaluation Criteria for IT Security, International Organization for Standardization, ISO/IEC 15408-1, December 2009. https://www.iso.org/standard/50341.html
CertiPath KR	*CertiPath Key Recovery Policy*, CertiPath, December 2013. https://www.certipath.com/downloads/20131216%20CertiPath%20KRP%20v.1.5.pdf
CP X509 CP	*CertiPath X.509 Certificate Policy*, CertiPath, Version 3.26, November 2014. https://www.certipath.com/downloads/CertiPath%20CP-v.3.26_final.pdf
	X.509 Certificate Policy for the United States Department of Defense, Department of Defense, Version 10.5, January 2013. https://iase.disa.mil/pki-pke/Documents/unclass-dod_cp_v10-5.pdf
	Key Recovery Policy for External Certification Authorities, Department of Defense, Version 1.0, June 2003. https://iase.disa.mil/pki-pke/Documents/unclass-eca_krp_v1-4_jun03_signed.pdf
FBP	*X.509 Certificate Policy For The Federal Bridge Certification Authority (FBCA)*, Version 2.31, Federal Bridge Certification Authority, General Services Administration, June 2017. https://www.idmanagement.gov/wp-content/uploads/sites/1171/uploads/FBCA-Certificate-Policy-v2.31-06-29-17.pdf
	Federal Public Key Infrastructure Key Recovery Policy, Version 1.0, October 6, 2017. https://www.idmanagement.gov/fpki/
	National Institute of Standards and Technology (1999) *Data Encryption Standard (DES)*. (U.S. Department of Commerce, Washington, D.C.), Federal Information Processing Standards Publication (FIPS) 46-3. https://csrc.nist.gov/publications/detail/fips/46/3/archive/1999-10-25
	National Institute of Standards and Technology (2019) *Security Requirements for Cryptographic Modules*. (U.S. Department of Commerce, Washington, D.C.), Federal Information Processing Standards Publication (FIPS) 140-3. https://doi.org/10.6028/NIST.FIPS.140-3
FIPS 180	National Institute of Standards and Technology (2015) *Secure Hash Standard (SHS)*. (U.S. Department of Commerce, Washington, D.C.), Federal Information Processing Standards Publication (FIPS) 180-4. https://doi.org/10.6028/NIST.FIPS.180-4

National Institute of Standards and Technology (2013) *Digital Signature Standard (DSS)*. (U.S. Department of Commerce, Washington, D.C.), Federal Information Processing Standards Publication (FIPS) 186-4.
https://doi.org/10.6028/NIST.FIPS.186-4

National Institute of Standards and Technology (2004) *Standards for Security Categorization of Federal Information and Information Systems*. (U.S. Department of Commerce, Washington, D.C.), Federal Information Processing Standards Publication (FIPS) 199.
https://doi.org/10.6028/NIST.FIPS.199

National Institute of Standards and Technology (2006) *Minimum Security Requirements for Federal Information and Information Systems*. (U.S. Department of Commerce, Washington, D.C.), Federal Information Processing Standard (FIPS) 200.
https://doi.org/10.6028/NIST.FIPS.200

Federal Information Security Modernization Act of 2014, Pub. L. 113-283, 128 Stat. 3073.
https://www.govinfo.gov/app/details/PLAW-113publ283

Booth H, Regenscheid A (2014) Reference Certificate Policy. (National Institute of Standards and Technology, Gaithersburg, MD), Draft (2nd) NIST Internal Report (NISTIR) 7924. Available at
https://csrc.nist.gov/publications/detail/nistir/7924/draft

OMB Circular A-130, *Managing Information as a Strategic Resource*, 28 July 2016.
https://obamawhitehouse.archives.gov/sites/default/files/omb/assets/OMB/circulars/a130/a130revised.pdf

Presidential Decision Directive 63, *Critical Infrastructure Protection*, May 1998.
https://www.govinfo.gov/app/details/FR-1998-08-05/98-20865

Electronic Signatures in Global and National Commerce Act, Public Law 106-229, June 30, 2000.
https://www.govinfo.gov/app/details/PLAW-106publ229

PL 113-274   Cybersecurity Enhancement Act of 2014, Pub. L. 113-274, 124 Stat. 3989.
https://www.govinfo.gov/app/details/PLAW-113publ274

Housley, R and Polk, T; *Planning for PKI*; Wiley Computer Publishing; New York; 2001.

Internet X.509 Public Key Infrastructure Certificate Policy and Certification Practices Framework, Internet Engineering Task Force, Network Working Group, Request for Comments 3647, The Internet Society; November 2003.
https://datatracker.ietf.org/doc/rfc3647/

Internet X.509 Public Key Infrastructure: Certification Path Building, Request for Comments 4158, September 2005. https://doi.org/10.17487/RFC4158

Internet X.509 Public Key Infrastructure Protocol (KMP), Internet Engineering Task Force, Network Working Group, Standards Track, Request for Comments 4210, September 2005. https://doi.org/10.17487/RFC4210

GSAKMP: Group Secure Association Key Management Protocol, Internet Engineering Task Force, Network Working Group, Standards Track, Request for Comments 4535, June 2006. https://doi.org/10.17487/RFC4535

Cryptographic Token Key Initialization Protocol (CT-KIP), Internet Engineering Task Force, Network Working Group, Standards Track, Request for Comments 4758, November 2006. https://doi.org/10.17487/RFC4758

Guidance for Authentication, Authorization, and Accounting (AAA) Key Management, Internet Engineering Task Force, Network Working Group, Standards Track, Request for Comments 4962, July 2007. https://doi.org/10.17487/RFC4962

Cryptographic Message Syntax (CMS) Authenticated Enveloped-Data Content Type, Internet Engineering Task Force, Network Working Group, Standards Track, Request for Comments 5083, November 2007. https://doi.org/10.17487/RFC5083

The Transport Layer Security (TLS) Protocol, Version 1.2, Internet Engineering Task Force, Network Working Group, Standards Track, Request for Comments 5246, August 2008. https://doi.org/10.17487/RFC5246

Certificate Management Over CMS (CMC), Internet Engineering Task Force, Network Working Group, Standards Track, Request for Comments 5272, June 2008. https://doi.org/10.17487/RFC5272

CMS Symmetric Key Management and Distribution, Internet Engineering Task Force, Network Working Group, Standards Track, Request for Comments 5275, June 2008. https://doi.org/10.17487/RFC5275

Cryptographic Message Syntax (CMS), Internet Engineering Task Force, Network Working Group, Standards Track, Request for Comments 5652, September 2009. https://doi.org/10.17487/RFC5652

Secure/Multipurpose Internet Mail Extensions (S/MIME) version 3.2 Message Specification, Standards Track, Request for Comments 5751, January 2010.
https://doi.org/10.17487/RFC5751

Trust Anchor Format, Internet Engineering Task Force, Standards Track, Request for Comments 5914, June 2010.
https://doi.org/10.17487/RFC5914

Use of the RSA-KEM Key Transport Algorithm in the Cryptographic Message Syntax (CMS), Internet Engineering Task Force, Standards Track, Request for Comments 5990, September 2010.
https://doi.org/10.17487/RFC5990

Internet Key Establishment Protocol Version 2 (IKEv2), Internet Engineering Task Force, Standards Track, Request for Comments 5996, September 2010.
https://doi.org/10.17487/RFC5996

Portable Symmetric Key Container (PSKC), Internet Engineering Task Force, Standards Track, Request for Comments 6030, October 2010.
https://doi.org/10.17487/RFC6030

Cryptographic Message Syntax (CMS) Symmetric Key Package Content Type, Internet Engineering Task Force, Standards Track, Request for Comments 6061, December 2010.
https://doi.org/10.17487/RFC6031

Dynamic Symmetric Key Provisioning Protocol (DSKPP), Internet Engineering Task Force, Standards Track, Request for Comments 6063, December 2010.
https://doi.org/10.17487/RFC6063

Algorithms for Cryptographic Message Syntax (CMS), Internet Engineering Task Force, Standards Track, Request for Comments 6160, April 2011.
https://doi.org/10.17487/RFC6160

Certificate Management Over CMS (CMC) Updates, Internet Engineering Task Force, Standards Track, Request for Comments 6402, November 2011.
https://doi.org/10.17487/RFC6402

RFC 6960   *X.509 Internet Public Key Infrastructure Online Certificate Status Protocol – OCSP, Updates,* Internet Engineering Task Force, Standards Track, Request for Comments 6960, June 2013.
https://doi.org/10.17487/RFC6960

Internet Key Exchange Protocol Version 2 (IKEv2), Standards Track, Request for Comments 7296, October 2014.
https://doi.org/10.17487/RFC7296

The Transport Layer Security (TLS) Protocol Version 1.3, Internet Engineering Task Force, Standards Track, Request for Comments 8446, August 2018.
https://datatracker.ietf.org/doc/rfc8446/

National Institute of Standards and Technology (2019) *Risk Management: Risk Management Framework (RMF) Overview*. Available at
https://csrc.nist.gov/projects/risk-management/rmf-overview

SP 800-15　　　Burr WE, Dodson DF, Nazario N, Polk T (1998) MISPC Minimum Interoperability Specification for PKI Components, Version 1. (National Institute of Standards and Technology, Gaithersburg, MD), NIST Special Publication (SP) 800-15.
https://doi.org/10.6028/NIST.SP.800-15

SP800-18　　　Swanson MA, Hash J, Bowen P (2006) Guide for Developing Security Plans for Federal Information Systems. (National Institute of Standards and Technology, Gaithersburg, MD), NIST Special Publication (SP) 800-18, Rev. 1.
https://doi.org/10.6028/NIST.SP.800-18r1

Kuhn DR, Hu VC, Polk WT, Chang S-j (2001) Introduction to Public Key Technology and the Federal PKI Infrastructure. (National Institute of Standards and Technology, Gaithersburg, MD), NIST Special Publication (SP) 800-32.
https://doi.org/10.6028/NIST.SP.800-32

Joint Task Force (2018) Risk Management Framework for Information Systems and Organizations: A System Life Cycle Approach for Security and Privacy. (National Institute of Standards and Technology, Gaithersburg, MD), NIST Special Publication (SP) 800-37, Rev. 2.
https://doi.org/10.6028/NIST.SP.800-37r2

SP 800-52　　　McKay KA, Cooper DA (2018) Guidelines for the Selection, Configuration, and Use of Transport Layer Security (TLS) Implementations. (National Institute of Standards and Technology, Gaithersburg, MD), Draft (2nd) NIST Special Publication (SP) 800-52, Rev. 2.
https://csrc.nist.gov/publications/detail/sp/800-52/rev-2/draft

Joint Task Force (2017), Security and Privacy Controls for Information Systems and Organizations. (National Institute of Standards and Technology, Gaithersburg, MD), Draft NIST Special Publication (SP) 800-53, Rev. 5.
https://csrc.nist.gov/publications/detail/sp/800-53/rev-5/draft

SP-800-53A　　Joint Task Force Transformation Initiative (2014) Assessing Security and Privacy Controls in Federal Information Systems and Organizations: Building Effective Assessment Plans. (National Institute of Standards and Technology, Gaithersburg, MD), NIST Special Publication (SP) 800-53A, Rev. 4, Includes updates as of December 18, 2014.
https://doi.org/10.6028/NIST.SP.800-53Ar4

Barker EB, Chen L, Roginsky A, Vassilev A, Davis R (2018) Recommendation for Pair-Wise Key-Establishment Schemes Using Discrete Logarithm Cryptography. (National Institute of Standards and Technology, Gaithersburg, MD), NIST Special Publication (SP) 800-56A, Rev. 3. https://doi.org/10.6028/NIST.SP.800-56Ar3

Barker EB, Chen L, Roginsky A, Vassilev A, Davis R, Simon S (2019) Recommendation for Pair-Wise Key-Establishment Using Integer Factorization Cryptography. (National Institute of Standards and Technology, Gaithersburg, MD), NIST Special Publication (SP) 800-56B, Rev. 2. https://doi.org/10.6028/NIST.SP.800-56Br2

Barker EB, Chen L, Davis R (2018) Recommendation for Key-Derivation Methods in Key-Establishment Schemes. (National Institute of Standards and Technology, Gaithersburg, MD), NIST Special Publication (SP) 800-56C, Rev. 1. https://doi.org/10.6028/NIST.SP.800-56Cr1

SP 800-57 Pt1   Barker EB (2016) Recommendation for Key Management, Part 1: General. (National Institute of Standards and Technology, Gaithersburg, MD), NIST Special Publication (SP) 800-57 Part 1, Rev. 4. https://doi.org/10.6028/NIST.SP.800-57pt1r4

Barker EB, Dang QH (2015) Recommendation for Key Management, Part 3: Application-Specific Key Management Guidance. (National Institute of Standards and Technology, Gaithersburg, MD), NIST Special Publication (SP) 800-57 Part 3, Rev. 1. https://doi.org/10.6028/NIST.SP.800-57pt3r1

SP 800-67   Barker EB, Mouha N (2017) Recommendation for the Triple Data Encryption Algorithm (TDEA) Block Cipher. (National Institute of Standards and Technology, Gaithersburg, MD), NIST Special Publication (SP) 800-67, Rev. 2. https://doi.org/10.6028/NIST.SP.800-67r2

Barker EB, Barker WC (2018) Recommendation for Key Establishment Using Symmetric Block Ciphers. (National Institute of Standards and Technology, Gaithersburg, MD), Draft NIST Special Publication (SP) 800-71. https://csrc.nist.gov/publications/detail/sp/800-71/draft

SP 800-88   Kissel RL, Regenscheid AR, Scholl MA, Stine KM (2014) Guidelines for Media Sanitization. (National Institute of Standards and Technology, Gaithersburg, MD), NIST Special Publication (SP) 800-88, Rev. 1. https://doi.org/10.6028/NIST.SP.800-88r1

Chen L (2009) Recommendation for Key Derivation Using Pseudorandom Functions (Revised). (National Institute of Standards and Technology, Gaithersburg, MD), NIST Special Publication (SP) 800-108, Revised.
https://doi.org/10.6028/NIST.SP.800-108

Barker EB, Smid ME, Branstad DK, Chokhani S (2013) A Framework for Designing Cryptographic Key Management Systems. (National Institute of Standards and Technology, Gaithersburg, MD), NIST Special Publication (SP) 800-130.
https://doi.org/10.6028/NIST.SP.800-130

SP 800-131A   Barker EB, Roginsky A (2019) Transitioning the Use of Cryptographic Algorithms and Key Lengths. (National Institute of Standards and Technology, Gaithersburg, MD), NIST Special Publication (SP) 800-131A, Rev. 2.
https://doi.org/10.6028/NIST.SP.800-131Ar2

Sönmez Turan M, Barker EB, Burr WE, Chen L (2010) Recommendation for Password-Based Key Derivation: Part 1: Storage Applications. (National Institute of Standards and Technology, Gaithersburg, MD), NIST Special Publication (SP) 800-132.
https://doi.org/10.6028/NIST.SP.800-132

Barker EB, Roginsky A (2019) Recommendation for Cryptographic Key Generation. (National Institute of Standards and Technology, Gaithersburg, MD), Draft NIST Special Publication (SP) 800-133, Rev. 1.
https://csrc.nist.gov/publications/detail/sp/800-133/rev-1/draft

SP 800-135   Dang QH (2011) Recommendation for Existing Application-Specific Key Derivation Functions. (National Institute of Standards and Technology, Gaithersburg, MD), NIST Special Publication (SP) 800-135, Rev. 1.
https://doi.org/10.6028/NIST.SP.800-135r1

SP 800-152   Barker EB, Branstad DK, Smid ME (2015) A Profile for U.S. Federal Cryptographic Key Management Systems (CKMS). (National Institute of Standards and Technology, Gaithersburg, MD), NIST Special Publication (SP) 800-152.
https://doi.org/10.6028/NIST.SP.800-152

SP 800-160   Ross RS, Oren JC, McEvilley M (2016) Systems Security Engineering: Considerations for a Multidisciplinary Approach in the Engineering of Trustworthy Secure Systems. (National Institute of Standards and Technology, Gaithersburg, MD), NIST Special Publication (SP) 800-160, Vol. 1, Includes updates as of March 21, 2018.
https://doi.org/10.6028/NIST.SP.800-160v1

SP 800-171   Ross RS, Dempsey KL, Viscuso P, Riddle M, Guissanie G (2016) Protecting Controlled Unclassified Information in Nonfederal Systems and Organizations. (National Institute of Standards and Technology, Gaithersburg, MD), NIST Special Publication (SP) 800-171, Rev. 1, Includes updates as of June 7, 2018.
https://doi.org/10.6028/NIST.SP.800-171r1

SP 800-175A   Barker EB, Barker WC (2016) Guideline for Using Cryptographic Standards in the Federal Government: Directives, Mandates and Policies. (National Institute of Standards and Technology, Gaithersburg, MD), NIST Special Publication (SP) 800-175A.
https://doi.org/10.6028/NIST.SP.800-175A

Barker EB (2016) Guideline for Using Cryptographic Standards in the Federal Government: Cryptographic Mechanisms. (National Institute of Standards and Technology, Gaithersburg, MD), NIST Special Publication (SP) 800-175B.
https://doi.org/10.6028/NIST.SP.800-175B

Department of the Treasury Public Key Infrastructure (PKI) X.509 Certificate Policy, Version 2.9, United States Department of the Treasury, March 15, 2017.
https://pki.treas.gov/docs/treasury_x509_certificate_policy.pdf

Key Recovery Policy for The Department of the Treasury Public Key Infrastructure (PKI), Version 1.0, United States Department of the Treasury, August 24, 2009.
https://pki.treas.gov/docs/dot_krp.pdf

Information technology – Open Systems Interconnection – The Directory: Public-key and attribute certificate frameworks, International Telecommunications Union Telecommunication Sector, ITU-T X.509, October 14, 2016.
https://handle.itu.int/11.1002/1000/13031

Appendix E—Revisions

The original version of this document was published in August 2005. Several editorial corrections and clarifications were made, and the following more substantial revisions were made in 2019 (Revision 1):

1. The Authority section has been updated.

2. Consistent with the Cybersecurity Enhancement Act of 2014 (PL 113-274), Section 1 now states that this Recommendation is intended to provide direct cybersecurity support to the private sector as well as the government-focused guidance consistent with OMB Circular A-130 (OMB 130). The revision states explicitly that the recommendations are strictly voluntary for the private sector, and that requirement terms (**should/shall** language) used for some recommendations do not apply outside the federal government.

3. The Glossary section was updated to improve consistency with recent publications. The following terms were updated: *accountability, certificate revocation list, client node, communicating group, compliance audit, compromised key list, cryptographic keying relationship, cryptographic key management system, de-registration (of a key), emergency key revocation, encrypted keying material, internet key exchange, Kerberos, key agreement, key-center environment, key certification hierarchy, key derivation, key distribution center, key generation, keying material, key recovery agent, key wrapping key, manual key distribution, mesh, message authentication, multiple-center group, peer, rekey, revocation, revoked key notification, service agent, suspension, transport layer security, token, trust anchor,* and *user* were added. The *association, asymmetric key algorithm, cryptographic key component, data key, data encrypting key, data origin authentication, dual control, encrypted key, integrity detection, integrity restoration, key de-registration, key management infrastructure, key registration, label, random number generator, secret key, security services,* and *subject certification authority* terms were deleted. The definitions for *authentication, authentication code, certification practice statement, confidentiality, digital signature, encrypted keying material, key processing facility, key transport, key update, key wrapping, non-repudiation, password, private key, public key,* and *X.509 certificate.*

4. The acronyms section was revised to add *CKMS, IKE, IPsec, Part 1, Part 2, Part 3, RKN, S/MIME,* and *TLS*; and delete KMI, *PRNG,* and *RNG.*

5. The term *key management infrastructure (KMI)* was replaced throughout the publication with *cryptographic key management system.*

6. References to TLS 1.0 and TLS 1.1 were deleted. A reference to TLS 1.3 was added.

7. In order to achieve consistent terminology with SP 800-152, the term Key Management Policy (KMP) was replaced throughout the document with Cryptographic Key Management System Security Policy (CKMS SP), and the term Key Management Practices Statement (KMPS) was replaced by Cryptographic Key Management System Practice Statement (CKMS PS).

8. Section 2 was updated to introduce a more comprehensive set of key management concepts that must be addressed in key management policies, practice statements and planning documents by any organization that uses cryptography to protect its information. The

revised section reflects guidance provided by SP 800-130 and SP 800-152, and broadens the applicability of its recommendations to cover both decentralized and centralized key management structures. The example centralized infrastructure design was replaced with explanatory material that reflects SP 800-130 and SP 800-152 and applies to both centralized and decentralized key management structures. The references to the now outdated RFC 4107 were deleted.

9. In section 3.1.2.1 and Appendix B, the requirement that the keying material manager also be the certification authority was deleted.

10. The original Section 4 (*Information Technology System Security Plans*), which provided documentation requirements for General Support Systems and Major Applications, was deleted as out of date.

11. For the second draft of *Part* 2, the document was re-organized to provide key management planning guidelines as Section 3, followed by guidelines for Key Management Specification (Section 4), Key Management Policy documentation (Section 5), and development of key management practices statements (Section 6).

12. The original Appendix A, *Notional Key Management Infrastructure*, was removed as outdated and bound strictly to hierarchical structures. It was replaced with a *CKMS Examples* Appendix A that describes both PKI and Center environments.

13. The original Appendix B was deleted. It is not necessary to repeat material from the IETF RFC 3647 standard.

14. The original Appendix C, *Evaluator Checklist*, was removed due to SP 800-130, *A Framework for Designing Cryptographic Key Management Systems*, and SP 800-152, *A Profile for U.S. Federal Cryptographic Key Management Systems*, now being available to provide the guidance covered in that appendix. Further, as stated in SP 800-53A, security control assessments and privacy control assessments are not about checklists, simple pass-fail results, or generating paperwork to pass inspections or audits—rather, such assessments are the principal vehicle used to verify that implemented security controls and privacy controls are meeting their stated goals and objectives.

15. The original Appendix D became Appendix C, and the original Appendix E became Appendix D.

www.ingramcontent.com/pod-product-compliance
Lightning Source LLC
LaVergne TN
LVHW081701050326
832903LV00026B/1852